Contents

Introduction: What is Meditation?   vii

1   Pakua: Walking Meditation   1
2   History and Mystery   6
3   The Benefits of Pakua Training   15
4   The Circle   33
5   The Pakua Animals   41
6   Momentum, Supervision, Inertia   47
7   Pakua Chang: Making the Changes   54
8   The Essential Ingredient   86
9   Taoist Philosophy   92
10 Pakua and the *I Ching*   103
11 Taoist Meditation   116
12 Beyond Theory   123
13 Ways of the Dragon: Applications of Pakua   136
    Conclusion   145

    Appendix: Complete Eight Palm Changes   150

    Glossary of Terms   156
    Further Reading   159
    Useful Addresses   160
    Index   162

Walking Meditation

PAKUA – THE MARTIAL ART OF THE I CHING

Paul Crompton

ELEMENT
Shaftesbury, Dorset • Rockport, Massachusetts
Brisbane, Queensland

Text © Paul Crompton 1996

First published in Great Britain in 1996 by
Element Books Limited
Shaftesbury, Dorset SP7 8BP

Published in the USA in 1996 by
Element Books, Inc.
PO Box 830, Rockport, MA 01966

Published in Australia in 1996 by
Element Books Limited
for Jacaranda Wiley Limited
33 park Road, Milton, Brisbane 4064

Cover design by the Bridgewater Book Company
Page design by Roger Lightfoot
Typeset by Footnote Graphics, Warminster, Wilts.
Printed and bound in Great Britain by Biddles Ltd
Guildford & King's Lynn

British Library Cataloguing in Publication
data available

Library of Congress Cataloging in Publication
data available

ISBN 1–85230–897–4

Introduction: What is Meditation?

Meditation, as a word, derives from the Latin *mederi* which in turn is related to the English words *medical, mode,* and *measure*. *Mederi* had the meaning of 'to attend to' in much the way a medical person attends to a patient. It can also mean 'to reflect upon'. The first meaning, of attending to or paying attention to, is the more apt of the two as far as our subject is concerned, despite the fact that 'meditation' is nowadays used to describe a number of different techniques rather than an act of paying attention. This has come about through a common tendency – one that we all share – of not seeing the wood for the trees. So, for example, to repeat a certain word, or mantra, is referred to as an act of meditation. The act of repeating the word is seen as meditation in itself. Alternatively, there is the practice of becoming aware of one's breathing and (for instance) counting the number of inhalations and exhalations. This too is called meditation.

But neither of these things, nor any other technique, is in itself meditation. Repeating a word is repeating a word; counting breaths is just counting breaths. What is important is the act of paying attention, with as much awareness of the act itself as one can muster. Mantras, breaths, heartbeats, shining candles – it is all the same.

The results of these methods can be very similar. The person may become quiet, more relaxed, and there may be a change in the blood circulation, in the skin surface, and in the type of brain waves taking place. All these things can happen without any technique at all: they happen to people who have never heard of meditation, let alone been trained at it.

If we want to be clear about this word, then, we have to put aside reliance on a particular technique, and put aside any results. Both obviously exist and are taught and spoken about, and the results are, of course, beneficial and even therapeutic – that is not in question in the least. Very many people all over the world have benefited from 'meditation'.

To clarify this, let us take something more easily understood – breathing. Everyone breathes. In a sense it is a life-giving, natural technique, if that is not a contradiction in terms. Everyone is very happy to have the results of breathing – they go on living! They can do all the things they do. But the act of breathing is not the same as the results.

What has happened to all the people who 'meditate' is that by trying a new technique they have been obliged, in varying degrees, to pay attention. Our major difficulty in appreciating this and giving it its rightful due is that 'paying attention' is such a common expression, and everyone 'knows' exactly what it is. And we can rarely give the right credit to something that we take for granted! Experience shows, however, that to pay attention is a very difficult thing. As the poet said, 'The good we never miss we rarely prize.'

Most people can pay attention to something that interests them, but far fewer can do so when something bores them or is completely outside their fields of interest. For anything outside such fields our attention span is weak and undeveloped.

Bringing these thoughts to bear on our own subject of Pakua, often known as Walking Meditation, we can ask what our field of interest is. Above all it is our body movement, and the sensations that accompany this body movement. This sensation-movement spectrum, so to speak, is one on which we are trying particularly to focus our attention, for Pakua is one of the inward-looking martial arts. The primary point is to pay attention; the secondary point is what we are attending to: our own 'psychosoma'. Our choice of focusing on the psycho-soma (the body–mind) is a good one, because it is a part of ourselves. Additionally, this focus is being done in the light of certain principles expressed in the Yin-Yang philosophy and in the trigrams of the seminal *I Ching* or Book of Changes.

Meditation as referred to throughout this book is thus the paying of attention to oneself. The question we all need to ask, without hope of an answer, is: what does this mean? It is easier to say what it is not. It is not thinking about oneself, feeling something about oneself, or imagining or visualizing something about oneself. It is more like listening to an impressive piece of music, feeling quiet while doing so, and then focusing this 'listening' on one's body and movements in a similar way. You might try this to understand what is meant more clearly.

When we refer to 'meditation' from time to time in the text, it is this that we will mean. Paying attention is fundamental. Neither Pakua nor any other martial art discipline can be done without it. Paying attention comes first, middle and last.

In Pakua we are paying attention to movement, new movement, and by doing this we discover new things about ourselves, and new possibilities. The combination of focusing attention on movement, combined with relaxation, brings about a result that is a new calmness, a feeling of assurance, and a sense of harmony. Although the results of meditation can be so to speak 'accidentally' experienced by anyone, it is the strong point of meditation that it is intended to produce just these results. It is not accidental.

Some people who meditate do so in order to have strange experiences. In my view this is better avoided. Strange experiences merely complicate life – which is already complicated enough. What is better to look for from meditation is greater simplicity. Meditation should make one feel more like a human being. I cannot define it, but we can all recognize the experience.

Chapter 1

Pakua: Walking Meditation

There are hundreds of Chinese martial arts and ways, which all differ from one another. One major distinction between them is the degree of muscular effort required. Another distinction is the amount of emphasis placed on awareness of the body – that is, on the attention given to the movements. For instance, Tai Chi Chuan is sometimes called 'meditation in movement', which implies a maximum of attention focused on movement, and a relaxation that is absent from many other Chinese martial arts. These are eventually accompanied by a kind of super-vision of the flow of *chi* (vital energy). *Yin* is soft, female, and *Yang* is hard, male. Using this classification we could say that the arts range from the most Yang to the most Yin, remembering at the same time that nothing is pure Yang or pure Yin.

The more Yin inwardly-turned arts are usually described as 'internal', and the more Yang the 'external'. Such expressions are very broad shorthand for what is in fact a complex subject – complex partly because of the difficulties of (and occasional mistakes in) translation, and also because of the problems inherent in applying so wide a concept to the flow of life. Tai Chi, Pakua and Hsing-I are often called the 'three internal arts', but there are others, such as Pa-Chi (the Eight Ultimates). These three are simply the best known. Tai Chi is the softest, Pakua somewhat harder, and Hsing-I is generally considered the hardest of the three. But Tai Chi can be very Yang, as in the Chen style, and Pakua can be performed with more emphasis on the Yin. For the most part it is the performance emphasizing the Yin that is presented in this book, for the reason that softness of movement can be more readily combined with the turning of the attention inwards: thus, the use of the term Walking Meditation.

Pakua is translated as 'Eight Diagrams (or Trigrams)': *Pa-* 'eight', *-kua* 'diagram'; in modern Chinese romanization the word is written *Bagua*. The trigrams referred to are those of the *I Ching* (see page 104). Pakua is also known as the Art of Walking the Circle, for walking in a circle using special footwork is a major characteristic. Yet again, Pakua may be called the Art of the Eight Palm Changes, corresponding to eight trigrams, because studying changes in movement is one of the most important aspects, and the open palms, in various configurations, predominate over the use of the closed fist. From the martial point of view, some practitioners say that the palm is more damaging than the fist.

While Tai Chi training and study has expanded by leaps and bounds in the Western world during the last decade, Pakua has lagged behind in popularity. This has been due to the shortage of willing teachers and, it must be said, a lack of promotion notable in the small literary output in the English language. But as more people take up the art, and more foreign and domestic instructors appear, that problem is being remedied, and a ripple of interest is already growing into a wave.

Many students of Tai Chi are not attracted to – and indeed are repelled by – the word *martial* and the associations conjured up by it. But that is a misunderstanding in relation to the Chinese martial arts. Martial arts are a discipline, even a way of life, that is reinforced by ideas and concepts, philosophies and moral precepts, which have their roots in the teachings of Lao-tze, Confucius and Buddha. Martial arts also incorporate theories and practical knowledge from traditional Chinese medicine.

As the interest in Pakua extends, people will perceive it to be on a par with Tai Chi in its diversity, its philosophical content, its promotion of health, and its martial applications. Teachers of dance, sports and gymnastics, and therapists who employ movement, not to mention other similar specialists, will find it useful to be acquainted with Pakua, for the methods of movement it proposes are probably unique, and certainly highly interesting. Martha Graham, the famous teacher, dancer and choreographer, said that she wanted to show what the human body can do, and that dancers are the 'acrobats of God'. She also said that there was only one freedom in her school, 'the freedom of discipline'. Yet at the same time, as an innovator in the modern dance field she was throughout her long career from 1926 to 1990 inspired by the theme of change. Such an approach is characteristic of the better Pakua masters. They have explored and expanded on the fundamental movements of their art since the early days.

Exploration is also very characteristic of Pakua training, in which students are taught a particular sequence of movements as a foundation and then invited to investigate the possibilities inherent in the sequence. One of my own teachers, Ji Jian Cheng, often said to me that Pakua is a freestyle form. This is in keeping with aspects of the *I Ching*, the Book of Changes, which played a big part in the formation of Pakua, as we shall see. There are established interpretations of the trigrams of the *I Ching*, but a student of the book must also learn to form his or her own. Similarly, although there are established forms of movement in Pakua, there remain possibilities for individual interpretation and variation.

It depends on what we might call 'movement intelligence' – an expression I have invented to mean a kind of watchful, alert sensitivity that comes from a specific part of the nervous system. Its psychological counterpart is summed up in the adage 'Rules are for the observance of fools, and the guidance of wise men'. If Pakua is more of a freestyle art, then the rules are there indeed for the guidance of students. Any departure from a set way of moving is valid if it fulfils the same aims as the original. 'Movement intelligence' can sometimes perceive this and make modifications accordingly. This is plainly different from making a modification out of ignorance or adding flourishes to a movement for the sake of showing off. If, for example, a sequence of movements has been produced by a small, thin, wiry person, one of whose pupils is a tall, fat, heavy man, then the latter may find that he is unable to perform in the same way as his teacher. Instead of struggling to do the impossible, his movement intelligence may show him how to adapt what he has learned to his own physique. One cannot be content with a sloppy performance that derives from mental and physical laziness.

Of course we are running ahead of ourselves here. Pakua

does have set forms, set positions for the head, arms, trunk and legs, and the first step is to learn them. The *I Ching does* have its eight trigrams and 64 hexagrams and the established interpretations, which also should be studied if a pupil wishes to associate his or her training in Pakua with that seminal book. The joints and muscles must become accustomed to new ways of working before any thought of improvisation. Work comes before play.

Aspects of the animal kingdom featured in the development of Pakua in terms of the qualities of movement and spirit which certain animals convey. Learning to move like a snake, students experience something about themselves that is certainly new. Similarly the movements of the seven other animals featured present psychological challenges. The task is to get inside the skin of each animal – and outside of one's own skin, as it were.

More than one Chinese martial arts expert has praised Pakua as a means of understanding and performing Tai Chi better. It is seen in particular as an excellent method of 'training the waist'. Pakua requires a close study of turning and twisting, which can help Tai Chi students to do such movements better in their own art. Like Tai Chi, the martial art of Pakua can be undertaken in a mood of tranquillity; any bellicose implication in the word *martial* is merely incidental. When I was learning basic Hsing-I from the same Ji Jian Cheng, and told him it was too tough for me in my early fifties he just said, 'Do it like Tai Chi.' So I did; and when it seemed possible, inserted the occasional stronger movement. Pakua can be done at slow or moderate speed, savouring the new type of movement, linking it with the *I Ching* and the animals, with never a thought of palming an adversary in the liver!

Tai Chi is frequently studied for health and tranquillity. It can bring a steady flow of energy, smoother breathing, and evenly paced action. Pakua is focused on *change*. In both arts one has to 'let the body move'. Joan Dexter Blackmer, a dance student of the Martha Graham company, and also a graduate of the CG Jung Institute of Zurich, wrote a thought-provoking book called *Acrobats Of The Gods*. She stated:

> In space, dance is organized by using countless combinations of basic geometric elements. Straight lines, angles, diagonals, triangles, squares, crosses, circles, spirals . . . these familiar patterns of the psyche provide the spatial structure for the danced image.

What is interesting in this extract is the idea that geometrical, spatial patterns are external shapes found in the human psyche. In this respect we may reflect on such ordinary expressions as, 'My thoughts just went round in a circle,' 'I felt cornered,' 'What's his angle?', 'I approached the problem in a roundabout way,' and so on. In these we imply that there is a similarity between what happens in the space-time world and in our brains, our emotions, our psyche. By following these different shapes with the body, we subject the body to *change*. At first, as we have said, these changes are learned, perhaps with difficulty, without inspiration, even doggedly. But once the movements are known, the changes lose their initial challenge and we can begin to get inside them, inside ourselves, and experience the effects of the physical changes on the psyche itself. We see that the two are closely linked – that there is a continuity between body and psyche.

Such experiences can readily be tested by simply describing a circle in the air with an open palm, moving at a slow, constant speed. The mental focus combined with the circular action induces a feeling of calm. In contrast, to move a hand in sharp, erratic and jagged figures produces a feeling of agitation.

If you take up Pakua and learn it correctly, you will discover not only new, pleasurable and exhilarating movements, but new subtleties of feeling and outlook which either correspond to the movements or which are evoked by them.

Chapter 2

History and Mystery

Pakua has found it hard to escape the almost universal mystery surrounding the origins of the Chinese martial arts. One reason for this mystery lies in the Chinese attitude to one's antecedents combined with a deeply ingrained respect for the ancients, for what came before. Consequently, any time the question of when a martial art began is raised – indeed, any time reference is made at all to the historical records – the inevitable proviso is appended, that an older date may be the correct date, according to some, and that a wise Buddhist or Taoist or Confucian or famous general or sage was the *real* founder of the art. If such an elevated personage was the founder, the art itself is similarly elevated, worthy of far greater respect than an art produced by a mere cobbler or footsoldier or starving unknown scholar.

Many followers of the Shaolin schools of Kung Fu attribute the founding of their arts to the Buddhist sage Bodhidharma. Followers of Tai Chi give the same accolade to the Taoist immortal Chang San Feng. That there is scholarly doubt about the very existence of such men, and that there is no conclusive contemporary documentation, are factors that are discounted altogether by the majority of martial artists.

Nevertheless, students of the history of Pakua have been exceptionally persistent in their quest for the truth. Certain points have been universally agreed: 1 Pakua derives partly from the Taoist stream of Chinese culture; 2 Pakua is related to the *I Ching*, the Book of Changes; and 3 Pakua contains Yin-Yang theory and philosophy.

Many students believe that Tung Hai Ch'uan, born in 1797, was the founder of Pakua. Tung's historical background is fully documented, and according to Professor K'ang Ko-Wu, a Beijing historian, this in itself lends credence to their beliefs. In preparing a thesis on the origins of Pakua, K'ang examined nearly 900 different documents, spoke to more than 400 teachers from all over China, and formally interviewed more than 250 people. Not surprisingly, K'ang found discrepancies in the claims made by the people he interviewed, notably in connection with a theory that Tung did not invent Pakua himself but based it on another martial art, Yin Yang Pa P'a Chang, which he learned from Tung Meng-Lin. K'ang concluded that this theory had no real foundation. (His reasoning for this is tortuous and more suited to a Court of Law than this book, but it does underline K'ang's thoroughness and the importance attached to lineage by the Chinese in general.) In my own experience of martial arts, the first thing a Chinese student or teacher will ask you is, 'Who was your teacher?' If he or she has not heard of that person before, the next question will be, 'Who was his teacher?' And so on. If he or she is personally satisfied with your tutorial lineage, you stand a chance of being taken seriously; if not, you will probably be treated with mere politeness!

A second theory was also knocked on the head by K'ang's investigations. This was the notion that Pakua derives from Pa Fang Pu or Eight Direction Stepping. K'ang concluded that the basic training methods of Pa Fang Pu were not the same as those of Pakua, and that this was good enough reason for discounting the theory. Some students do not agree with this conclusion. Much of this type of argument is of course based on certain assumptions. For instance, it is reasonable to assume that if the basic training of one art is not the same as that of a later art, that later art could not have derived from the earlier one – but this is not to accept the possibility that in changing the primary tenets the basic training could also have been changed. On the other hand, if both the primary tenets and the basic training have been changed, why look for any connection, let alone similarity? To appreciate much of what is said in this regard it is necessary to some extent to be an 'insider' – that is, to have studied martial arts and been through the mill of trying to get to the bottom of certain questions. This is how to get a nose for things, just as one can in any specialist subject.

Another theory was that Tung Hai Ch'uan learned Pakua

from a Taoist somewhere up high in remote mountains; the
Taoist's name was said to be Pi Ch'eng-Hsia. Now the 'Taoist in
the remote mountains' is a commonly repeated scenario, and
is uncritically and widely accepted because of the flavour of
mystery-and-history it imparts. This notion was also discounted
by K'ang. He therefore came to the decision that Tung himself
produced Pakua. Of course not everyone agrees with him, but
even those who disagree base most of their reasoning on his
research. I know of no one else who has done research on this
subject with the same thoroughness. Prior to K'ang's efforts, the
information was scattered about China and no one in the public
eye was in a position to make a judgement based on such a
breadth and depth of data.

The question then arises: On what did Tung base his new art?
The story is that Tung had already learned other martial arts
and had studied also with Taoist monks who had several
methods of moving and walking in circles and segments of
circles as part of their meditation exercises. His genius was to
combine all this material into a whole. To a martial artist this is
a feasible and historically justifiable claim. Yin Fu, one of
Tung's most highly regarded pupils, was an expert in Lohan
Ch'uan prior to turning to Pakua, and he later used Lohan techniques in his Pakua. The founder of Aikido, Morihei Uyeshiba,
drew from a miscellany of sources. Jigoro Kano, the originator
of Judo in the first half of the 20th century, did likewise. Bruce
Lee explored many arts and came up with his famous Jeet Kune
Do approach. Korean arts such as Hapkido and Taekwondo are
amalgams of earlier methods. So there are plenty of examples of
men who studied widely, studied a variety, and produced
either something new or something with an emphasis on a
particular aspect that was so formidable as to be described as
new.

When Tung began to teach, he inevitably set in motion a process of divergence from his original art. One of his earliest
pupils was Cheng T'ing Hua. Another was Ma Wei-Chih. These
men taught others, and as time passed, the first- and second-
generation pupils stamped their individual marks on Pakua,
giving rise to various styles. This is a common feature of
Chinese and Japanese martial arts. For instance, in the widely
studied art of Japanese Aikido, pupils of the founder, such as
Saito, Tohei, Tomiki and Shioda, each gave Aikido a personal

emphasis or style. Tohei was more interested in studying Ki (*chi* 'power'), whereas Tomiki turned Aikido in a sporting and educational direction, possibly influenced by his strong background in Judo.

As Pakua spread through the country and down the generations, greater and greater diversity appeared. Sun Lu Tang, who was also a skilled Tai Chi and Hsing-I exponent, introduced movements from the latter art into his Pakua. His movement sequence called Swimming Dragon – which I studied myself with Ji Jian Cheng – contains a number of Hsing-I techniques blended into the Pakua techniques. Pakua also 'emigrated' to Korea in the person of Lu Shui-Tian. From the mid-1960s, a number of European and North American students travelled to China, Hong Kong and Taiwan to study with the contemporary teachers: they included such men as Jerry Alan Johnson, Joseph Crandall, Vince Black, Dan Miller and Bruce Frantzis.

Today, in both Europe and North America it is thus possible to find a diversity of styles of Pakua. Chinese teachers of the various styles visit fairly frequently, and the official Chinese Athletic Committee promote their own version of the art as part of an accepted syllabus of martial arts training. Such versions in turn undergo modifications. The latest version of this form that I have seen closely resembles the Old Fu style of Pakua, as produced by Fu Chen Sung, a pupil of Cheng T'ing Hua and Chia Ting Te.

In my experience it is fair to say that the more exacting methods of training used by the teachers of the 19th century and the early decades of the 20th are for the most part looked upon as curiosities: few modern instructors use them. Such methods are frequently cited to show what martinets for discipline the old teachers were, and how the students of today have 'gone soft' compared with their predecessors. For example, how many modern students would be prepared to study one posture, one physical position, for a whole year, before going on to another one? Sun Lu Tang, and later, Chang Chun Feng, are known to have undergone this type of prolonged discipline as part of their training. And they were not alone in this. Standing in one position, or sitting, is a feature both of Chinese martial arts training and of Chi Kung (internal energy cultivation).

A second feature of training – both in bygone days and currently – is rising very early, at 4am for instance, in order to practise. And when training is over it is followed by a day's work!

A third feature of all martial arts and Chi Kung training was, and to some extent still is, secrecy. Chang Chun Feng kept certain aspects of his own Chi Kung training secret even from his wife . . . though he did eventually relent and teach her. Reasons for trying to preserve the esoteric nature of martial arts training include:

- preventing a competitor or enemy from knowing your methods;
- keeping things 'in the family', and so stopping people of bad character from becoming skilful;
- maintaining a sense of respect for the art itself;
- full supervision to make sure each student proceeds at a suitable pace and does nothing that might be injurious.

Of course it is impossible to say just how far this secrecy was maintained, but one of my own teachers told me that he was chatting to his brother-in-law, having known him for years, at a family occasion, and the brother-in-law was amazed to find that he, my teacher, was a martial artist.

Along with other arts, Pakua has been studied mainly by illiterate people, and by comparatively few scholars. Over the centuries the Chinese people have looked down on martial artists: for a martial artist also to be well educated came as a shock to those who made such a discovery. It was Sun Lu Tang who first brought the martial arts of his generation before the public by writing a number of books that were well researched and presented. But hearing that Sun was well versed in the classics, one scholar refused to believe it; it was only when he saw Sun's calligraphy that he realized he had been mistaken. Sun was famous for his studies of the *I Ching* and for his efforts to relate it to the martial arts, and in particular to Pakua.

Chiang Jung Ch'iao was another famous martial artist and scholar, whose first and preferred art was Mi Tsung Ch'uan. With characteristic thoroughness he researched the history of this art and became an innovator in the sense that he revived aspects of the art that had largely been lost. At the time, during the first half of the 20th century, the Chinese government was making efforts to raise morale and improve the overall health of the nation. Chiang made sterling efforts to boost this movement, and founded organizations to promote health, fitness and martial skills, while also writing and publishing books on all these subjects. Discovering Pakua, Chiang began to study it, putting the same intensity into it that he had used in studying Mi Tsung Ch'uan. He passed away in 1974, leaving behind an enriched system which his pupils have maintained ever since. His most notable pupil was Sha Kuo Cheng, who died in the early 1990s.

Because the majority of martial artists were not well educated, they preserved the wisdom of their arts through the careful study of movement and the experiences and impressions that came from such studies. They did not have the wherewithal to write down, analyse and codify their methods. The noted martial artist and teacher Yang Jwing-Ming several times pointed out that this lack of education led to the passing on of instructions for the cultivation of *chi* (vital force) that could only be approximate, because the students did not know the correct *chi* channels and acupuncture points. That such obvious anatomical approximations were used was also due partly to the fact that many students trained solely in order to fight, testing and perfecting techniques that would defeat an adversary in combat. But throughout the history of the martial arts a thread has run that has linked them with the theories and methods either of Taoism or of Buddhism, and perhaps with Shamanist teachings from Mongolia and the all-pervading rural life of China. Every rural community had elements of knowledge that were known simply from daily contact with the land, handed down from time immemorial. There is therefore a strange blend of refined sensitivity and extreme violence in Chinese martial arts. Velvet hands in iron gloves, and iron hands in velvet. There is also an instinctive and intellectual awareness of the planet, as in Feng Shui or geomancy, combined with an unsurpassed grasp of warfare and politics. All in all, an amazing world.

Many martial artists, including Pakua students, came from a rural background. Life was harsh in ways which most modern Westerners would find it hard to imagine. For instance, it happened not infrequently that a student had to leave his village because there was famine and people were dying for lack of food. Or that a student worked simply for food and shelter, not for money, such was the tenor of the times. A young man in these straits was Chang Chao Tung, born in 1859. He went from the country to the town and eked out a living demonstrating his martial arts in the street. His early experiences in life had given him a strong dislike of anyone who threw his weight about, including criminals, and he took it upon himself to squash the pretensions of such people. His activities in this regard brought him to the attention of the authorities, and he was given the job of an arresting officer.

Although no longer officially permitted, fights for money, prizes and prestige were common at that time. A student or teacher of one style of martial art would challenge someone of another style, and the bout would take place in public. Sometimes the outcome was the death of one of the participants. There are several stories of how Japanese, German and Russian strong men, wrestlers and martial artists challenged Chinese – and it goes without saying that if a Chinese defeated a foreigner, his reputation increased mightily. This theme, with variations, has continued to feature regularly in martial arts movies, including those of Bruce Lee.

There are also many stories about the miraculous powers of Pakua practitioners, especially concerning their amazing agility. The ability to leap several metres into the air, to walk the circle with such speed that the feet almost do not touch the ground, to walk up vertical walls, and even to walk upside down on ceilings, are all described in the martial arts annals. Such tales are discounted even by living relatives of the martial arts masters, including the daughter of Sun Lu Tang, who was interviewed by American journalist Dan Miller in 1993 in Beijing. In a way, of course, it does not matter whether they are true or not; they enliven the art and place emphasis on its direction and on its characteristics.

But two stories about Sun Lu Tang are authentic. On one occasion he was in a room full of students. Asked to demonstrate his skill he challenged them to touch him. Despite the fact that there was little space in the room, none of those present managed to lay a finger on him. The other story centres on an exercise that the reader may like to try out for himself. Sun stood with the edge of his foot touching the base of a wall, and his shoulder and arm on the same side in contact with the same wall – so that for example his right arm and shoulder and the edge of his right foot touched the wall. He could then raise his left knee up to be level with his waist and remain in contact with the wall without losing his balance to the left. Can you? When asked how he did this, he replied that the centre of gravity of his body was wherever he wanted it to be.

The martial art most often spoken about in the same breath as Pakua is the art of Hsing-I Ch'uan or Body Mind Boxing. Several Pakua and Hsing-I masters crossed swords, figuratively speaking, during their careers, and the outcome of such encounters was usually one of mutual admiration and respect. Some of the fundamental movement-sequences (Forms) in Pakua can be seen to incorporate Hsing-I techniques. It was also a practice in the case of some Hsing-I teachers to train students in their own art and then send them off to study with a Pakua master in order to refine their movements and to afford them the liveliness and speed of the brother method.

In this book, which attempts to relate Pakua as Walking Meditation, to an increased awareness of the body in movement; the extraordinary power that some practitioners develop is not emphasized. It is there, potentially, in the gyrating actions of the body. But the development of power is best left to the living classroom and an experienced teacher. If Pakua goes the way that the bulk of Tai Chi training has gone, then within a few years many dozens of 'teachers' will have appeared in the West. One Tai Chi organization was reported in 1995 as giving students six-week courses and then letting them loose as teachers. They must have had extraordinary aptitude!

If you are looking for a teacher of Pakua, therefore, try to find out something of his tutorial lineage – that is, from whom he learned, and for how long. Also, if your prospective teacher has a background in other martial arts as well, you could pursue enquiries in that direction too. In my experience, first teachers make a big, possibly even indelible impression, producing habits of movements, correct or incorrect, that are difficult to change or erase. If you work with a teacher whom you admire and with whom you can develop a warm relationship of trust, however, even bad first habits can eventually be ironed out. A point worth emphasizing further is not to leave your common sense at the door. Never argue face to face with a Chinese *sifu* (teacher) because it will cause him or her to 'lose face'. Think about things for yourself, try them out, and then ask polite questions.

As my own pupils know, the way I do martial arts has changed over the years. This has come about through a combination of seeing better martial artists than my own first teachers and doing my own research. Part of this research has involved paying attention to what I called 'movement intelligence' earlier in this book. By listening to your body very carefully you can learn things about how you are moving. Doing this, I slowly altered the way I did certain movements. Later, when I saw Ji Jian Cheng moving, I found that some of the ways in which he moved corresponded with the changes I had subjectively made. I felt gratified. You may well find the same thing happens for you.

Chapter 3

The Benefits of Pakua Training

Although Pakua is a Chinese Art, and its benefits can be described in terms of Traditional Chinese Medicine (TCM), this chapter discusses them using Western terminology. The famous Taoist Yin Shih Tzu, who studied and wrote about meditation throughout his life, gave up using Chinese terminology at the age of 31. In 1954 at the age of 82 he wrote that he preferred 'using scientific terms and analysis to describe the theory of meditation' (*Tranquil Sitting*, Dragon Door, 1995). It is also a mistake, in my view, to mix the two terminologies because the underlying ideas and concepts are different. For instance, the concept of *chi* (*qi*) has been described as bioelectric energy. This is too vague. Bioelectric energy is used all over the body and is not limited to what TCM calls *chi*.

A 'YOUNGER' SPINE: CRANIOSACRAL THERAPY

The spine consists of vertebrae, nerves and cerebrospinal fluid. The neck vertebrae are described as cervical, the chest vertebrae thoracic, the mid-section vertebrae lumbar, and the pelvic vertebrae sacral, plus the 'tail' or coccyx. The thoracic and cervical vertebrae permit some rotation, but the lumbar and sacral remain relatively stable in the horizontal plane. All the vertebrae are capable of some flexion and extension: see figure 1. This illustration shows the natural curvature of the spine. With this curvature, the spine supports the rest of the body. Imagine a force pushing down vertically on the top of the head, representing the gravitational pull of the contents of the head, the

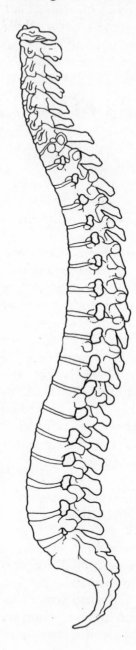

Figure 1 Spinal column showing natural supportive curve

heaviest part of the body per cubic centimetre. The curvature acts like a spring, so that the spine can give and 'rebound'. If the spine was absolutely straight, there would be little possibility of springiness and any suddenly-applied force might snap the spine.

If the spine is lopsided or wrongly curved in any plane, it acts like a truck that is unevenly loaded. The weight of the body, and of anything you might be lifting or carrying, produces an uneven stress on one or more parts. Pakua can promote the correction of such misalignment. It also cultivates the springiness of the spine through frequent turning movements which are part of the art. It also helps to ward off the usual processes of ageing.

Surrounding the brain, encased in the skull, to the extremity of the spinal column, there is a 'bath' of cerebrospinal fluid (CSF) which cushions the nerves and structures against shock, reminiscent of how an embryo is protected by fluid in the womb. One of the significant features of CSF was brought to the attention of Western physicians only a few decades ago. It led to the establishment of new types of therapy called Cranial Osteopathy and Craniosacral Therapy. Most people know that osteopaths manipulate the joints of the body when things go wrong with posture. Many of us have experienced the dramatic click of a joint movement and, hopefully, the immediate relief. The pioneers of Cranial Osteopathy studied the possible slight movements in the bones of the skull, a form of treatment that produced amazing results in a variety of different cases.

The joints of the skull bones are referred to as sutures, and there are 34 of them: they can be found in any detailed book on anatomy. An important point of disagreement between some members of the orthodox Western medical profession and the followers of the Craniosacral Therapy fraternity is the question of whether the bones of the adult skull are fused and therefore fixed, or whether there is some discernible movement between the joints of the bones of the skull. This is a crucial question for the whole basis of the unorthodox argument because if the bones of the adult skull are fused, movement and changes in pressure of the CSF would make no palpable impression on those bones.

Craniosacral Therapy (CST) holds that the secretion of CSF causes a rhythmic pulse to be conveyed through the fluid at a rate of 6 to 10 times per minute. Each cycle in which the pulse goes out and returns causes change or fluctuation in pressure that is transmitted throughout the whole body by means of the body fluids and the membrane tension. CST finds arguable analogies between this pulse and the many pulses of nature and of human activity, and refers to the action of the pulse in the same terms as those applied to muscle use: extension and flexion. A further effect of the pulse is held to be related to the idea of coiled energy in the martial arts and the absence of *chinglo* (acupuncture channels) which spiral or coil along the limbs.

The theory is thus that the flexion caused by the pulse urges the two sides of the body to rotate along longitudinal axes externally and with the extension phase internally. CST claims that in the spinal cord itself the outgoing fluid wave travels down in a coiling or spiralling fashion with a tendency to spread onto other fluid and membrane areas. Because most organs and body parts are surrounded by some form of separating membrane, this fluid wave effect is transmitted everywhere. In connection with the meridian theory of acupuncture, some CST practitioners maintain that the *chinglo* or meridians pass along the membranes of the organs and limbs.

Most of the activity of the body described here is not outwardly visible: it can only be felt (palpated) by an experienced practitioner. This tends to be one of the causes of disagreement between orthodox and unorthodox parties. The same potential for disagreement formerly existed (and to some extent still does) in relation to acupuncture. It should be said, also, that some proponents of CST do wax very lyrical about their subject, as is characteristic of all enthusiasts, and this too alienates the more orthodox critics. Every CST practitioner reckons to have a highly-tuned organism that he or she can use as an instrument to diagnose the state of the CSF of patients. Their bodies are like a human stethoscope that focuses on the homeostasis of the patient: homeostasis – the tendency of the body to try to maintain the status quo – is an important element in CST because practitioners see the craniosacral system as a delicate barometer of the body's overall condition. One key to this condition is the state of the pulse and the membrane tension.

A fundamental tenet of CST is that unpleasant stress is stored in the membranes of the body. It is axiomatic, therefore, that emotional stress and the body tissues interact, and that when the emotions cannot cope with an upsetting event or situation the body reacts to this in its own way, producing tendencies that are then stored up. In the membranes these take the form of two different patterns, one a 'holding pattern' and the other a 'breakdown pattern'. The holding pattern is concerned with reactions to emotional stress, and the breakdown pattern with reactions to physical trauma. One feature of these patterns is that they may persist long after the initial causes have disappeared. It is part of the work of the practitioner to find and release them; in a way this is analogous to the process of psychoanalysis.

All I want to do here is to make the connections between CST and the methods and notions found in the martial arts and Chi Kung. What martial artists and Chi Kung practitioners have done is to take elements of such philosophies, whether in modern Western sources or early Chinese medical sources, and attempt to apply them to movement. The all-important premise for this application is that body movement can influence CSF and the membranes and connective tissues of the body. Such influence is applied at several levels: one level is that revealed by the sensitivity of the CST practitioner, although there may possibly be a higher level of sensitivity, and there certainly are differing levels of lower sensitivity. A secondary premise is that a person can do this for himself or herself, and does not need the assistance of a hands-on therapist.

The primary premise is naturally accepted by CST, but from its point of view the secondary premise needs investigation. It does not need investigation into its overall truth, because there is plenty of evidence from practitioners of genuine yoga, Zen Buddhists and others that CSF can indeed be influenced by the individual alone. What does need investigation is the level of sensitivity needed to influence the CSF *safely*. Some martial arts teachers have lighted on the word *pump* as used to describe the creation of the pulse referred to earlier. It is possible that the notion of a pump has been taken too literally. The pulse of CST is something very delicate, invisible to the eyes of most of us, and so its visible effects when compared to the movement of a limb through space are slight. Whether physical movement of a relatively gross nature, compared with the microscopic adjustments of the therapist's hands, can in reality influence the pulse of the CSF is therefore something that needs clarification. Even if it were found to be true, the next question would be whether it is advisable. The cyclic pulse operates at a rate of between 6 and 10 cycles per minute – but this obviously varies from person to person. How would a martial artist be able to tell at what rate he or she should perform the proposed movement of the back for instance? What would be the basis for the decision? If an unsuitable cycle were introduced, what would be the effect?

The CSF enters the body at the lower half of the brain and empties into a reservoir just below the surface of the brain, after being dispersed towards the base of the spine. We have to assume that the intelligence of the body decides on the rate at which this is done. If a martial artist arbitrarily changes the pulse rate, would it be beneficial, and why? Whatever else, it must be sensible – if not essential – that a period of preparation is undergone before any attempt to change is made. Part of this preparation should be to 'get in tune' with the intelligence of the body before lending a hand.

Not all martial artists or martial arts teachers are interested in this type of question. Some just want results, energy, physical power. The possible side effects are of little interest to them. To me this seems unwise.

Cranial Osteopathy now similarly has a respected place in Western medicine. One of the applications of this work has been the treatment of young children with sleep and behavioural problems such as constant crying for no observable reason. Positive results have been reported. There is worldwide evidence that the methods produce good results in people of all ages. Many general physicians as well as osteopaths have been trained in the therapy.

In the United States, Pakua students with a medical background claim that Pakua training promotes the movement of CSF in a beneficial way, curing a variety of problems. Basically, this is a question of mobility. As we age, the spine loses its resilience and mobile qualities: Pakua can help to preserve these properties. It is the same with spinal osteoarthritis. As we age, the intervertebral discs begin to lose their fluid content and consequently their capacity to recover. The shock absorbers become less able to absorb shock. This leads to a flattening of the discs and an eventually distinct loss in height. The body fights back by producing muscle spasm and pain, in its attempt to reduce movement. Later, it begins to deposit calcium on the edges of the discs. These can fill in the joints and produce inflammation and even more pain from the pressure on the roots of the nerves.

Much of the damage and pain is caused by misalignment, but some of it derives through lack of use. The less you use something, the less usable it becomes. There is an old saying to the effect that a much used gate does not accumulate cobwebs: an active, well used spine is less likely to accumulate arthritis. Pakua training, correctly carried out, will help in this. If you observe older people, you will see that one of the types of movement that many of them are reluctant (perhaps even unable) to make is to turn and look over their shoulders. This is due to loss of the rotatory facility in the upper thoracic and cervical regions. In Pakua this rotatory type of movement is basic.

It is well known that as we age the restriction of our joints increases. But this is not inevitable. People may accept it as if it was, but it is not. Admittedly, we cannot use the same muscular force or the same extremes of joint stretching in our fifties as we did in our twenties. But we can remain physically active. Joints do have natural limitations dependent on their design and purpose. For example, the knee joint is not designed to rotate, just to bend. But other areas – for instance the shoulder blade or scapula – are capable of a very wide range of movement. If the sheet-like scapula is kept moving freely, the whole of the shoulder region, the pectoral girdle as it is called, will remain free. Shoulders will not become hunched or bunched, and the head and neck will not stay firmly locked in place.

If you attempt some of the arm and shoulder movements described in this book you will appreciate that Pakua uses just about every possible action of the scapula. Although you may find that you are not capable of doing some of the movements yet, with training and patience you will be. So we can remind ourselves that Pakua can be used for many purposes all useful to us: the martial aspect, the study of the *I Ching*, the cultivation of meditation in movement, in an exploration of new physical actions, and as a therapy.

ENDORPHINS

The word *endorphin* is now widely used. It is based on the word *morphine* and implies 'the morphine within' – that is, the 'morphine' produced within the body. But like Cranial Osteopathy, the very idea of such a thing was at one time restricted to a very few scientists. The struggle to prove the existence of endorphins was long and protracted, and they remain a subject of controversy. Briefly, endorphins are substances which, when released at nerve junctions (synapses), deaden or prevent the experience of pain. If there is no source of pain, their increase in the body can help to produce a more peaceful state.

Their discovery was part of a major effort on the part of scientists and drug companies to find a painkiller that was not part of the opium-based range of drugs. In 1973 the two major painkillers available to the public were aspirin and paracetamol (acetaminophen). Opiates were addictive; aspirin was thought to be relatively safe. But migraine, arthritis and chronic pain were beyond the reach of aspirin. So if someone could discover a non-addictive – that is, non-opiate – drug, a fortune could be made.

Earlier in the century, neurotransmitters (substances such as dopamine and serotonin) had been discovered. Although no certainty existed at that time as to how neurotransmitters worked, it was believed that certain 'receptors' for them accepted their 'messages' and produced a variety of effects. One example was a substance that could regulate the activity of the heart. These discoveries led researchers to think that whole classes of unknown chemicals might exist which would explain changes in mental states and physical conditions.

Endorphins have been described as constituting one such class. They have been proposed as one of the active factors in acupuncture anaesthesia, in which patients undergo major surgery without externally-applied anaesthetics. It is also suggested that endorphins are part of the body's natural resources to counter stress. Another widely held belief is that they are produced by any strong persistent exercise, and that this explains the 'high' which many people feel after a tough aerobics workout, or indeed any strenuous exercise.

But whereas aerobics or jogging, for instance, can result in bad and persistent injuries, there are forms of exercise which

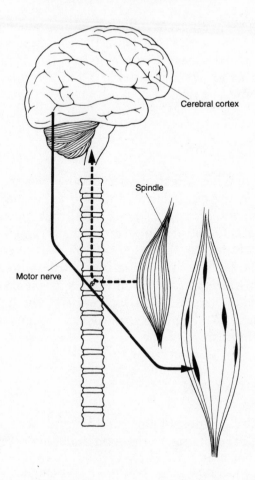

Figure 2 Stretch reflex diagram

need have no such results. Pakua is one of these. Done with care, done correctly, Pakua exercises the whole body, produces the so-called endorphin effect, and has no bad results. In addition, the unusual stretching movements that many dancers and athletes use as part of their training produce the 'stretch reflex'. This phenomenon takes place when a muscle is stretched. Muscles are so constructed that when they stretch there is an in-built tendency for the muscle to pull back in the opposite direction: see figure 2. When correctly performed, Pakua produces this reflex in many muscles and gives the student a sense of relaxation not otherwise usually experienced.

It almost goes without saying that all the benefits described so far have psychological effects in the sense of feeling better, feeling well, more at ease, better able to cope, stress reduction, and all the other expressions used to describe changes that most people welcome as a relief.

BALANCE

Nearly everyone has a fear of falling. Whatever the causes, we are afraid of losing our balance. But children are not afraid, and flop down on the ground without a murmur, even with pleasure. The intricate and flowing stepping movements of Pakua, combined with the unusual use of the body, the centralization of balance, the focus on the circle, all contribute to a much better attitude towards movement through space. Pakua is a discipline of constant change, not fixity. Fear is fixity, unwillingness to move. Once you begin to experience change, your fear of falling will diminish.

THE CIRCULATION

We can attribute much of the curative and health-improving results of Pakua training to the 'ebb and flow', the 'emptying and filling' that is improved circulation. Here we are referring for a moment to Chinese terminology, by which we mean Yin and Yang. Many aspects of disease are due in some measure to the breakdown or impairment of this complementary process. If you visit a large Western pharmacy or chemist shop and examine the medicines, you will find that in one way or the other many of them specifically improve circulation. The words on the labels may not say so, but the medicines work in that way. For instance, pain relievers can reduce pain by improving circulation. Laxatives cure the lack of 'circulation' in the bowel: emptying and filling. Medicines which help diarrhoea cut down on the over-active emptying. Those which free congested breathing help the circulation of the air in and out of the lungs and nasal passages. So in a general sense much of our health depends on the right working of some stop-go signals and performance. 'All work and no play makes Jack (and Jill) a dull boy (and girl).' You will find that regular and correct Pakua training will amply attend to this question of circulation.

Of course, no one system can cure or even help everything, and you must always consult a physician or osteopath or other specialist if you have something the matter with you. Do not stick your head in the Pakua sand!

EXTREMITIES

Many people suffer from cold hands and feet, especially in wintertime. It is frequently blamed on poor circulation. Perhaps from lack of exercise, such people's blood supply and the accompanying energy flow do not go out adequately to the hands and feet. In Pakua we would say that the soles of the feet and the palms of the hands are 'dead', lacking all sensitivity.

It was found during biofeedback experiments that if a person concentrates on the palms of his or her hands, in conjunction with an electronic apparatus which showed the temperature of the skin surface, that he or she could actually raise the temperature of the skin surface. This demonstrated clearly that we do not have to undergo laboratory conditions to carry out the experiment. As we have seen, Pakua requires that the feet and the hands are moved and placed in particular ways, and that at times the attention is focused more firmly on the palms and soles of the feet. Furthermore, the stretching of the palms and soles engages the muscles, tendons, ligaments and joints in the stop-go, flexion-extension, and wholly natural ebb and flow that any wild animal goes through daily. Because the hands and feet are the extremities of the body, any increased circulation and energy flow that reaches them must pass the entire length of the limbs, with resulting benefits to them also.

For people who are interested in healing methods that use the hands – in massage, acupressure, shiatsu, do-in, and so forth – the increase in sensitivity and strength that Pakua brings will be a welcome addition to their capabilities. Chinese Chi Kung emphasizes that full circulation is essential to health as it brings in the nourishing *chi* and sends out the used *chi*. Of course, as in most things, success depends on regular and correct training. There is no once-and-for-all big effect that permanently sets things to rights.

MIND AND BODY?

As a teenager in the late 1940s and early 1950s I studied Yoga
and read books on the philosophy of the Indian *Upanishads*. In
those days the division between mind and body was a firmly
established, relatively unquestioned tenet of Western thought.
When I came across the idea that for two systems to connect
with one another there must be a region of similarity, I was
very struck by it. We know that the 'mind' influences the
'body', and vice versa. There must therefore be some bridging
area across which these actions can take place.

Nowadays such ideas are fairly commonplace – yet we still
speak of the mind and the body as separate. Of course they are,
in a sense, but they make a whole. We cannot really think of a
human being without one or the other. Mind and body inter-
penetrate one another. Pakua, along with numerous other disci-
plines, makes use of this phenomenon. It does so through the
medium of *change*. Someone said that Time is what prevents
everything from happening at once – a provoking definition.
Change takes place in Time, and stress can be defined as react-
ing to a situation that does not exist *now*. If I miss a bus or train
and spend the next 30 minutes fuming and worrying about
missing an appointment, I am going on about something which
cannot be cured *now*. It will be cured in 30 minutes' time. If my
partner or spouse leaves me for some reason, I may cling to the
past and spend the rest of my life regretting it, remembering the
past. But that does not exist *now*. Change is inevitable.

There is a Zen story to the point. A Zen master attracted the
attention of a pretty young woman but showed no interest in
her. She made love to another man and conceived. When asked
who was the father of the child, she said that the Zen master
was. People told him about this. He said, 'Is that so?' Later the
young woman relented and told the truth. People told the Zen
master about the latest episode. He said, 'Is that so?' He lived in
the present and took each change as it came.

Pakua movement and philosophy is conducive to greater
adaptation or adjustment to change.

Returning to the interpenetration of mind and body, try the
following experiment. Use the muscles of your face to produce
a smile. Do it several times, and then hold the smile. You will
probably find that you begin to feel inside that you are smiling,

and that there is something to smile about. If you take the Pakua movements for the monkey, which can be light and playful, and perform them for a while, you will begin to feel light and playful, even though there may be nothing in your life at the moment to make you feel this way. Then switch to the powerful movements of the dragon. Your mood changes again. At the same time you may not want to change your mood, but the power of the movements will change it anyway.

You may object to this line of argument, saying, 'Well, this is all artificial. I don't really feel like a monkey or dragon. It is all contrived.' This is true, but it implies that your usual states of mind, your moods, are *not* contrived, that they are real and justifiable – in a phrase, that they are truly what you feel. This objection does not bear up under scrutiny. It is true that some states of mind are more real and genuine than others, but how many of them are? If you miss a bus and become angry, is this really you? If you are a man and miss your bus, turn round and find an attractive woman behind you waiting for a bus, and she smiles at you and shows an interest, you will forget your anger and instead be interested in the woman. So how real was your anger?

Pakua training can illustrate this and throw light on the subject of change in general. Just as animals are supposed to have adapted physically in order to survive, perhaps we have to learn to adapt psychologically, not only in big, global ways, but in moment-to-moment more trivial ways – that is, in ways that are part of our daily lives.

CASE STUDIES

The martial arts of the East contain notable examples of people who started out in life as weak, sickly children, and who then became immensely fit and strong. There are also cases of weak, sickly adults who became much healthier.

For example, the founder of Aikido, Morihei Uyeshiba, began life suffering constantly from ill health. Through martial arts studies he became immensely strong and fit, in addition to his skills. Koichi Tohei, a pupil of Uyeshiba, was also a weakling, a frail child. He followed in his teacher's footsteps in health, strength and martial ability. Cheng Man Ching, the world

famous Tai Chi master, is a further case in point. He suffered
from tuberculosis and he attributed his cure to the study of Tai
Chi under the master Yang Cheng Fu.

In Pakua, too, there is no shortage of health ambassadors. In
the United States there is Dr John Painter, well known to Pakua
students. Physicians told his parents that he might not live
beyond the age of 18. His childhood was a chronicle of ill health,
absence from school, and general misery. At the age of 11 he was
fortunate to meet an experienced Pakua practitioner and herbal-
ist from China, Dr Li Jiulong. For nine years he studied and
trained, following Dr Li's instructions, and almost from the start
his health began to improve. In his late forties he reported that
he owed almost everything in his life to Pakua training.

Bruce Kumar Frantzis is another American martial artist who
specializes in the internal martial arts. Some years ago he was
involved in a serious car crash which threatened him with
paralysis at worst and severely restricted movement at best.
Through a combination of Chi Kung and Pakua he was able to
reconstruct his body and his life. He now writes and teaches
without any restrictions on his physical activity.

Liu Yun Ch'iao, a Chinese martial artist born in 1909, was
also a child invalid. His two elder sisters had not survived their
childhood so his father was most concerned that his heir should
live to manhood. At the age of five he was 'handed over' to a
martial artist and bodyguard, Chang Yao Ting, who massaged
his body and trained him in martial arts. Liu grew into a
healthy youngster and later became a famous Pakua teacher.

Sun Lu Tang was a Tai Chi and Hsing-I master who also
excelled in Pakua. The Sun style of Tai Chi bears his name, and
a style of Pakua is named after him. His was a miserable and
poverty-stricken childhood. In his early teens his condition
drove him to attempt suicide from which he was rescued by
some passers-by. Martial arts restored meaning and success to
his life, and gave him the respect of his contemporaries and the
gratitude of later generations of students.

Avoiding Injury

Some years ago, before Ji Jian Cheng returned to Chengdu in
the People's Republic of China, we made a video programme of

him doing the Swimming Dragon Form from Sun Lu Tang's Pakua. In this programme he is shown, at times, doing the movements with the utmost vigour and exertion. The memory of this prompts me to issue a word of warning to beginners. *Do not try to copy an expert directly: you will injure yourself.*

As I have stressed in this book, aim to move softly and relatively slowly. An expert builds up the body, especially the joints, to be able to withstand the strain of strong turning movements. Such a development has to be even – the same everywhere. If one group of muscles is stronger or weaker than the rest, it will very likely contribute to an injury. Although injuries can occur anywhere in the body, in Pakua the ankles and knees and lower back are particularly vulnerable. In my own experience the ankles are important: I had an old ankle injury, and Pakua very quickly showed me that I could not forget it.

So a key word of advice is to move as one unit. Do not emphasize one part of a movement – for example, spinning on the balls of the feet – and play down the rest.

Begin by walking the circle, and as you walk try to be aware of all of your body. Be aware of the rhythm of your steps, and how this rhythm is experienced everywhere – from the soles of the feet to the crown of the head to the tips of the fingers. In this way you will more readily 'hear' warning signals from any joint or muscle that is having trouble keeping up. This simple endeavour, expressed in a few words, is a difficult undertaking, requiring patience and regular training.

As you walk and twist your torso slightly towards the centre point, occasionally release the twist to rest the muscles concerned. Also, change direction regularly so that you twist in the opposite direction. This will additionally ensure that your neck muscles are not 'held' in a frozen position.

As you walk, ease the shoulder, elbow, wrist and finger-palm joints so that they too are not frozen. This advice ties in nicely with overall advice to beginners about assuming that the first posture you take is correct. It is unlikely actually to be correct, so if you vary it for the sake of your muscles and joints you will also ensure that bad postural habits do not become established. Keep the 'idea' of what you should do, but move your body around it.

When you toe-in to make a V step or toe-out to make an open T step (heel facing instep), be careful with your knees. You may not be able at first to perform either of these two steps correctly. Do not force your joints into position. Be content with an approximation, remembering at the same time what the position should ideally be. The knees in particular are vulnerable with these two foot positions. Take them smoothly and within your capacity.

When you thrust one arm under the other, as in the Dragon Turns Its Head at the beginning and end of each Palm Change, do not use a lot of force. You could injure your chest (pectoral) muscles. Push your underneath hand into place firmly, in one unbroken movement.

In the Lion Holding a Ball movement, be careful of your lower back. Do not lean backwards as you raise the ball high. You do lean a little – but only a little. This is an expansive movement, and you could be carried away by it and have to be carried away! As in all your training, go carefully; be aware of the muscles, and if you feel a blockage, stop, relax, stretch, and try again.

It is not necessary to go through the whole of the Form giving isolated pieces of advice. Stay close to the idea of a soft Yin approach and you will be able to advise yourself. But if you should sustain an injury, cut short your training and seek expert medical advice.

It goes without saying that before taking up any martial art, if you have any doubts about your fitness you should consult a physician first.

Once you have some experience in Pakua and are no longer a beginner, in the technical sense, you may come across another phenomenon. This can be described as a kind of threshold. Let us say that you can do the Palm Changes competently, and your body experiences no difficulty. You feel confident. So you decide to speed up or use more force or go deeper and higher in your movements, or all of these.

Wait! This is just the time when you could injure yourself. In Tai Chi training it is a maxim of mine that you should always have some energy in reserve. You should have more energy than you need. You may not have, but it is what you are aiming for. Likewise in Pakua: when your energy level seems to be in excess of what you need to perform at your present stage of training, that is when you can think of extending yourself. Not before.

This is not an easy maxim to put into operation because the temptation is always to push yourself. It is fair to say that the maxim is part and parcel of good martial arts training in general. It is far easier to strain and push than it is to build up an energy reserve. To do this requires patience and self-restraint. It is like not flying off the handle emotionally if someone says something insulting to you or is getting on your nerves. If the building up of *chi* is feasible, as traditional theory maintains, then this practice I am suggesting is an example of it. It will also help to preserve you from injury. When you begin to feel you have excess energy during training, let it be. If it makes you feel uncomfortable, relax and walk about; massage your body from the head downwards to the feet. In a while the excess energy will dissipate, but when you train again it will somehow come back. With patient persistence you will have this extra energy more and more in your training. It will be like a warm blanket. It will be like something you wear, not something you want to be rid of.

When this becomes more established at the time of your training, it will then be the correct time to push yourself a little further in some aspects. By then you may not have the impression that you are pushing yourself but that you are experimenting – by which I mean that instead of wanting to achieve something, you will rather be interested in seeing if something more is possible, or 'what happens if . . .?' You will be less interested in the result and more interested in the process itself. To come to this will be a very good sign. It means that you are much less prone to injury, but in a way, more importantly, that you are beginning to really experience the benefit of approaching Pakua inwardly.

If you think about it, the Lesser Heavenly Circulation (for instance) can be taught to an impatient person. It is, in a sense, a mechanism. It can be taught to an impatient person and not necessarily make him or her more patient. Yet, if we want something positive from Pakua, it is in an overall sense. We do not want an isolated achievement, like being able to walk the circle faster than anyone else in the world! There is little point. A truly patient person will learn the Lesser Heavenly Circulation very quickly, and appreciate it. An impatient person may learn it and obtain very little benefit from it.

So if you develop a reserve of energy in training, and can

maintain it for a while, you will be less likely to injure yourself physically or psychologically. As one of my teachers used to say, 'I said it was simple; I did not say it was easy.'

Chapter 4

The Circle

The circle is a shape that has been used by human beings in many ways. It features in architecture of all types, in dances, in games, in philosophical syllogisms, in allegorical thinking and in many other areas of our lives. In theoretical mechanics, for instance, and in the practical application of mechanics to various types of machinery, the study of rotational (circular) forces is a fascinating subject. Even though few machines work at the slow speed of a walking man or woman, or even at the speed of a rushing Pakua expert, the forces at play are very similar.

If you walk in a circle, or better still run in a circle that has a wide diameter, you will have almost no sensation of what is called centrifugal force. That is, you will feel almost no outward force away from the centre for which you have to compensate. But if you walk (or run) in a circle that has a diameter of, say, 1 metre (3 feet), you will find that you have to keep twisting your body towards the centre of the circle, and turning your feet a little towards the centre as you step, in order to hold to the circle. You will probably do it automatically – that is, you will contract the appropriate muscles that will enable you to keep moving along the circumference. It is simple and interesting to try this exercise and see what you do.

Figure 3 shows a spiral diagram. If you start at point A and move along the spiral to point B, walking quickly, you will experience a growing need to twist your body towards the central point of the spiral. If you then tighten the curve to reach point C, the inward twist increases. This demonstrates the simple fact that the tighter the curve, the more turning-in force

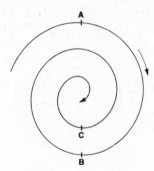

Figure 3 Spiral diagram

is needed to maintain it. This can be expressed in a simple rule:

> The sharper the curve, moving at a constant speed, the greater the turning-in force towards the centre.

Abbreviate these elements to C (curve), S (speed), and F (force). If C gets larger or smaller, F does likewise. If S gets faster or slower, F does likewise. If C and S either increase or decrease together, F does the same but to a greater degree than if only one of them changes. This may seem a rather academic approach at this stage, but remembering it when you come to do some Pakua may help you to move with more intention. For example, if you wish to move very quickly in a rotating fashion, it must be useful to know that you will need more turning-in energy to do so. Obviously, if you try this you will automatically feel it to be true. But if you know it in advance, it will help you to keep your balance.

I suggest that you try out the above variations again, and see for yourself what is meant. Use your ordinary way of stepping, and choose a circle of a set size. Then vary the speed of travel. Choose a tighter circle and try again. And an even tighter circle; and so on.

What you may notice also is that the faster you travel, and the more you have to turn inwards, the more tense you become. This is a usual and automatic reaction, but it should not be ignored or accepted. If it is, you will become overtired and your developing techniques will suffer. Above all, it is unnecessary, for quite simply, the main muscles in play at this stage are the leg muscles. So relax your torso and face, neck and shoulders, and focus on letting your legs and feet do the walking. Secondly, you might become dizzy. Just use your common sense about this, and gauge your capacity. It helps, of course, to change the direction from clockwise to anticlockwise and back again. Even a circle as wide as 3 metres (10 feet) can produce dizziness.

The Centre

In Pakua, the centre of the circle is a most important point. You may wish to place a small object in the centre of your circle so that you can keep in mind exactly where it is. With training, however, you should be able to tell where the circle's centre is without any external aid – and there are several reasons for this.

In psychological terms, the centre of the circle may be said to represent a sort of centre inside yourself. This idea is very widespread in both Chinese and Japanese martial arts. The internal 'centre' is often thought of as an actual region of the body, just below the navel: *tantien* (*dantian*) in Chinese, and *tanden* in Japanese. To the Japanese the whole of the lower abdomen is the *hara*, and it is on that location that one's attention should be focused. Not only can this be of psychological benefit but because the body's overall centre of gravity is roughly in this region such a focus gives more physical stability. The development of an awareness of this centre takes time and practice. It means that as you move, whatever you do, some awareness of the centre persists. It means also that your movements emanate from this region. Whatever the distractions outside yourself, and whatever thoughts or emotions may pervade you, you still maintain some awareness of the centre. Such an approach is a part of some Zen and other Eastern methods of meditation.

As you walk the circle(s) of Pakua, in the primary way described above, spend a minute or so keeping some awareness of the centre of the circle, and the centre in the lower abdomen. This will give you a sense of stability *as you move*. We tend to think of stability as a function of keeping still.

There is an interesting little experiment you might try in connection with awareness of an object in space. In the evening when it is dark outside, go into a room with which you are familiar, switch the light on, and put a pen or diary down on a table or on a shelf. Look at the object and the room for a few moments, then switch out the light so that you cannot see the object. Go to the other end of the room, turn around, then walk directly to the object, without hesitation, and pick it up. Put the light on again. Then stand at the table, put an object down on it, turn around, and reach behind you and pick the object up, without hesitation.

In both of these instances you should be able to pick up the object without faltering. Your body has the capacity to remember where objects are without reference to seeing or thinking where they are. This applies to the centre of the circle. You *know* where the centre is provided you do not interfere with the capacity of knowing.

Similarly, your body *knows* where the *hara* or *tantien* is, because it is making use of the knowledge at all times, when you are not lying down, as part of the balance-maintaining process. The question is how to refrain from interfering. It is much more difficult to do this than to be aware of the external centre of the circle. But Pakua provides a connection or link between the centre of the circle and the centre in your body. It is part of the next exercise.

Walk around a circle once again – say, one of 2 metres (6½ feet). Raise your inner hand (your right hand if you are walking clockwise) in the position shown in figure 4, so that your index finger is vertical and its inside, the palm side, faces directly towards the centre of the circle. It is like a sight on a rifle. As you walk, keep your index finger facing the centre at all times. Focus on the centre of the circle – and at the same time be aware of the lower abdomen. After a few cycles, turn and move in the opposite direction using the other arm. Your index finger links the two centres. At times, lower your arm, and try to retain the awareness of the two centres nonetheless.

These exercises can be demanding. Although you do not appear to be doing very much, the mental effort is telling and even tiring. With practice you will be able to maintain it longer, although even then your concentration will fluctuate. That is inevitable. You cannot expect to maintain unbroken, uniform awareness of anything, as has been experimentally proved. It has something to do with the fact that all life processes occur

Figure 4 Dragon posture, walking position

while undergoing some type of fluctuation, no matter how long or short these fluctuations may be. Of course the movements you make will gradually become easier, more habitual, and the need for serious effort will diminish. But, conversely, since an internal art is not aimed at cultivating habits but at cultivating awareness, you must not be lulled into falling asleep.

Practise regularly, be patient and don't give up.

The following exercises are offered to break up the monotony of training – should you find it monotonous. They also will prepare you for the Pakua Palm Changes which come later.

1) Walk the circle with arm and index finger upright as before. As you walk, bring the extended arm closer to your eyes, slowly, by bending your elbow, then push it out again, always focusing on the centre. Turn to walk in the opposite direction, extending the other arm, from time to time.

2) Walk the circle with arm and index finger upright as before. As you walk, bring the extended arm, still extended, away from the centre of the circle, across the perimeter of the circle, and out to the side. If you are walking clockwise, this means slowly swinging it from the right to the left, in a horizontal arc, and back again. Try doing this keeping your eyes on your index finger. Try it also keeping your eyes on the centre so that your arm is 'seen' in this case only by your peripheral vision.

3) Walk the circle clockwise, and after a few paces turn to your

right through 360 degrees, on the spot, and continue to walk. Repeat this, say, every half-circle you walk. Aim to recover your balance and land exactly on the perimeter. Do not circle out away from the perimeter or in towards the centre.

4) Walk the circle, and after every circuit shorten or lengthen your stride for the next circuit. Likewise after every circuit increase or diminish your speed for the next circuit. Experimenting in this way you may find a speed which appeals to you: it may vary from session to session, but in my experience there are speeds and circle sizes which seem to be the best for each occasion. 'Best' applies to those that offer the most possibilities. For instance, you may travel quickly but find that you cannot focus at such a speed. Or you may travel slowly and begin to daydream. A 'best' is something in which a compromise between as many factors as possible is found. Another way of putting it is to say that you feel comfortable but not dreamy.

5) This exercise breaks away from the circle-walking and begins to prepare your muscles for the Palm Changes. Walk the circle, and after a few paces step towards the centre, keeping your index finger focused on it. When you reach the centre, step away from it keeping your index finger focused on it: see figure 5. As you step in towards the centre the 'stretch' on the extended arm changes. That is, in stepping towards the centre the stretch of the muscles between the body and the arm diminishes as the angle between the arm and the body diminishes; and as you step away at the same angle the stretch increases. This will happen only if you keep

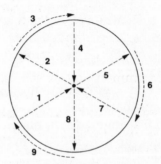

Figure 5 Centre in, centre out

your index finger focused on the centre. The reason the stretch diminishes and increases is because as you walk the circle your torso is turned in but the feet follow the circumference. As you step into the centre, however, the feet are in line with the torso, diminishing the stretch. As you step away from the centre, the feet face the new direction but the body is still twisted back towards the centre.

When you come to learn the Palm Changes you will see that this stretching of the muscles on the inside of the body at the index finger side is an important feature.

In general, the Pakua movements in this book are confined to the perimeter of the circle. In some Forms such as the Swimming Dragon of Sun Lu Tang there are movements from the art of Hsing-I meshed into the movements of Pakua. These cut across the circle in straight lines, and are included in the Forms for reasons of versatility and combat. That is to say, in the martial aspect of Pakua it can be useful to be able to break out of the circular movements and make a direct straight-line attack, and then just as suddenly move back into circular movements.

Such changes also train a student to be able to adapt mentally to a situation that would require them. If you continue to study Pakua and find the teachers to help you, it will become apparent that there are many borrowings and alterations from the original ideas. Fu Chen Sung, a pupil of Cheng T'ing Hua, was a widely experienced martial artist who eventually produced a Form of his own called Fu Dragon Palm. Some of the founder's original students additionally discovered a preference for certain techniques of Pakua which they stressed and developed for themselves, passing the results on to their pupils. It is fair to say that most original Pakua techniques and Forms have a strong emphasis on keeping to the circle, and that circular techniques are their hallmark.

It is nonetheless common among Pakua teachers to instruct students in techniques that rely on straight lines first. This is simply because straight lines are easier both from the point of view of learning and remembering, and from the point of view of physical performance. The author has not emphasized this, because the primary aim of this book is not combat but walking the circle, and finding and keeping a centre.

According to Pakua theory, the circle can be regarded as 'inhabited' by eight animals, in a formal association with parts of the human body. See the table on page 108. The circle is thus either empty, full of space, or populated by varying forces akin to those that constitute the body. If it is empty, it is like a painter's blank canvas, waiting to be occupied by the colours and shapes of your movement. If filled with force – the forces of the animals, for example – the 'model' is (so to speak) already there for you.

Chapter 5

The Pakua Animals

The number eight is an important number in Chinese culture and ideas, and it is not surprising to find it crucial in Pakua. There are eight animals, eight trigrams, and in the fundamental Forms there are eight Palm Changes. (Some styles of Pakua either do not have or do not emphasize the Forms so much as the Changes, as in the Yin Fu style.) In the layout of the trigrams in a circle there are the eight directions: north, south, east, west, and north-east, north-west, south-east and south-west, corresponding to the four major and four minor directions of the compass, as directly related to the very popular science of Feng Shui, or geomancy.

The eight animals are:

- snake
- dragon
- lion
- hawk
- bear
- phoenix
- unicorn
- monkey

Animals have been the inspiration of many martial arts, Chi Kung methods and approaches to Feng Shui. In other books and papers on Pakua, different words for the animals are sometimes used in translation, particularly for 'hawk', in relation to which the name of a different bird of prey occasionally features. There is no actual discrepancy.

If you were to imagine a scene in which these eight animals

were arranged in a circle, and that each was behaving in its characteristic fashion, you would certainly witness a great diversity of behaviour. What a strange and powerful impression it would present! Discounting the mythical nature of the dragon, phoenix and unicorn, there would be no place on earth, except in your imagination, where such a scene could be found. Not in the wild, not on film, not in a zoo, and not in a circus. Only the human mind would juxtapose such an array. If you pause for a moment and conjure up the picture, imagining the sounds, the movements and the contrasts, you will see that it presents you with eight images almost impossible to reconcile. Each is acceptable on its own, yet put the bear and the monkey together, for instance, and you feel that they do not fit. Together they produce a kind of tension. In nature each has its own domain, its own moods, its own way of life. In Pakua they are in the same circle. The art of Pakua relates them in movement.

We do not have to look very far, however, to find a unity that contains something akin to this apparent diversity – in fact only as far as our own human bodies. There we have a multiplicity of organs and a range of systems that are equally dissimilar. The kidneys filter and deal with watery fluids; the heart beats and pumps the blood; the lungs exchange the air; the testicles and ovaries contain the elements of new life; the liver cleanses the blood; the alimentary canal conducts food along the avenue of digestion; the different glands send their vital secretions into the bloodstream. Although all are serving the aim of continuing life, each is very different. All are housed in close proximity, yet each functions during health without impinging destructively on any other; on the contrary, each one supports the activities of the others.

It is characteristic of Chinese arts, including Pakua, to find analogies between one system and another. So the images and nature of the eight trigrams, the movements of Pakua, the organs or regions of the body, and the eight animals in question may all be referred to as one whole. Our Western view of the relationships between phenomena may not accord with the logic behind such an arrangement, but in Chinese culture it is an accepted approach. There is no need to seek links like this with what we call 'scientific proof'. Chinese thinking has a very strong element of working with precedent: what was right and wise before is right and wise now. We need look no further than the wisdom of our forebears and of the ancients. Are we wiser than they were? And so on. Although modern China is undergoing immense change, along with the rest of the world, Pakua still retains a great deal of the former ideas and teachings.

Each of the animals has a special place in Chinese cultural history. It is both interesting and relevant to outline their characteristics and to explain some of the ways in which they feature in the culture.

SNAKE

The Chinese ideograph for the snake is said to derive from a pictorial representation of a cobra, poised to strike. It is one of the animals of the Twelve Terrestrial Branches. These are part of a period of 60 years called the Cycle of Sixty, which is a method of naming and counting years and which allocates an animal to each, particularly used in Chinese astrology. The snake is a symbol of cunning, almost evil intent, yet it is looked up to with a degree of respect, even reverence. It was commonly believed that fairies and goblins changed themselves into snakes. Snake Forms or movement sequences are found in other martial arts systems. The respect paid to the snake does not prevent snakes from being killed and used in a variety of medicines.

DRAGON

The dragon is the emperor of the reptile family. There are theories about what dragons originally were, but of course no one has any historical evidence. One such theory is that the idea of dragons was inspired by alligators.

The dragon is renowned for its power, agility and magical ability to become invisible. Beneficence is one of its strongest characteristics, and one that distinguishes it from the demonic dragon of European tales. There are three types of dragon: the Lung that lives in the sky, the Li that lives in the sea, and the Chiao that lives in caves and marshes. Like the snake, the dragon is one of the animals of the Twelve Terrestrial Branches.

Since the year 206 BC, in the reign of Kao Tsu, the dragon has been the emblem of imperial power. The throne of the emperor, his garments, and many items of daily use in the imperial palace bore the symbol of the dragon. In more recent times, Bruce Lee had the nickname of Little Dragon!

There is a dragon style of Kung Fu, and in other martial arts there are dragon techniques, dragon stances, and so forth.

LION

Lions are sacred to Buddhism, and statues of them are often found guarding the entrances to Buddhist temples. In China, as elsewhere, the lion is regarded as the king of the cat family. Lions are not indigenous to China, and tigers – which are – are afforded more respect. Lion dances are performed to bring good luck to new enterprises, as are dragon dances, but as far as I know, not tiger dances. Lions are supposed to have a playful nature as well as courage and strength. Often in dances and martial arts methods they are shown playing with a ball. In Pakua we shall see this type of technique in the Eight Palm Changes.

HAWK

The words *falcon, harrier* or *sparrow hawk* may be used in Pakua writings as alternatives, and perhaps other terms applied to birds of prey – occasionally even the general word *raptor*. The interest in hawks was probably at its highest during the Mongol dynasties, for the Mongols were great lovers of hawking and falconry. Hawks were considered to be bold and keen-eyed. They figure widely in pictorial decoration, as used on banners for example. Their feathers were believed to be effective in curing smallpox. Speed and pinpoint accuracy are their hallmarks.

BEAR

The bear has several sides to his nature in Chinese martial arts. On the one hand he is powerful, well balanced and stable in his postures, slow and lumbering, but not incapable of speed. On the other he can be playful. He is renowned for his bravery. He is a symbol used on charms against thieves and burglars. The Five Animal Chi Kung sequence features the bear, giving him an ancient ancestry in this field. For all these elevated qualities, he does not escape belonging to the multitudinous range of Chinese foods: his paws are regarded as a particularly desirable delicacy.

PHOENIX

This mythical bird appears only in times of peace, when the people are thriving. It is one of the four intelligent and supernatural creatures of Chinese culture (the first is the dragon, the second the phoenix, the third the unicorn and the fourth the tortoise). Its domain is the warm south, for it was itself produced by the sun. Whereas the dragon appeared on the clothing of the emperor, the phoenix appeared on the clothing of the empress. Only one phoenix is ever seen at a time. When the country falls on evil times, it disappears. So peace and tranquillity are essential states for the phoenix to thrive.

UNICORN

A symbol of longevity, grandeur and happiness, the unicorn is said to be able to walk on water. Just before Confucius died, a unicorn appeared, and during the reign of the first legendary Emperor Fu Hsi, a unicorn came up out of the Yellow River with a mystic map on its back from which the written language of China evolved. Gentleness and benevolence are its hallmarks. Because humankind has degenerated since the days of the sages of China, no more unicorns have been seen on earth. Unicorns were depicted on the robes of military officials at the imperial court.

MONKEY

The monkey style of Kung Fu is well known to martial artists. There is the drunken monkey, the stone monkey and the monkey of the Five Animal Chi Kung. It is held to be ugly and devious. Because a monkey helped to guard some sacred Buddhist texts on their journey from India to China, the monkey was made into a god by the then Emperor, who gave him the title 'Great Sage equal to Heaven'. It was prayed to by many people as a help in driving away evil spirits. The monkey can bring health, protection, and success. In the martial arts its agility, fantastic physical dexterity and speed are legendary.

Chapter 6

Momentum, Supervision, Inertia

In the martial arts of Tai Chi and Wing Chun there is an exercise used in 'warming up' to relax the shoulders and arms. Although not performed in exactly the same way in both of the two arts, it is similar enough in each to warrant comparison, and in a modified form it can be used to induce relaxation in the turning and curving steps of Pakua. In figure 6 the student is standing in a Horse stance – keeping the legs in place, holding the weight centralized while turning from left to right, allowing the arms to swing as the movement of the torso gives them momentum and not through the use of the arm and shoulder muscles.

My experience as a teacher tells me that this explanation cannot be left as it stands! Most students cannot let the arms and shoulders go. The habitual use of the arm muscles in any activity in which the arms move at all makes it difficult to let go. So allow your arms to 'go dead', and your shoulders to 'go dead' too. Turn from the waist and torso, and let the arms swing freely. If you turn slowly they will move very little. If you build up speed they will swing much higher. Be careful not to overdo it, or you may strain hip and lower back muscles. Do not rotate the knees and ankles. Let the lower torso and legs produce the force for the action, and let the upper body do the turning.

When you have got the hang of this exercise, adapt it to the following Pakua series. Instead of standing in the horse stance in a static position, turn on the spot using something like the V and outward T steps, see figure 13. Let the arms go as in the static exercise, and they will billow out like mother's washing used to do on the clothes line on a gusty day. Make one rotation

Figure 6 Horse stance turning   Figure 7 V and T step turning
exercise

to the left, 180 degrees, and one to the right and repeat. See figure 7.

As you finish each 180-degree turn, your arms should fall to your sides if they are properly relaxed. If they do not fall, it means you are holding them up with your arm and shoulder muscles. As you V and T step round, sink down lower by bending your knees a little to give yourself more push, and to keep your balance. Once you have accomplished this movement satisfactorily, try to focus more and more on relaxation *as you turn*. You will then begin to experience directly how the lower body can be full and strong while the upper body and arms are empty and light. Keep your eyes on the horizon and your head upright.

An image that comes to mind in connection with arms swinging freely in this way is that of the roundabouts of various types at fairgrounds. When the roundabout is still, the chairs or seats hang down vertically on their rods or chains, just like your arms. As the central axis, your body, begins to rotate, the chairs begin to move out away from the centre. As the axis increases its speed the chairs swing out even further. If the speed is then kept constant, the angle between the chains and the axis remains constant. The chains have no energy of their own: it is all provided by the axis rotation. So it may help you if imagine that your arms are the chains on a roundabout. Pay attention, though, as you decrease your speed, to letting your arms relax and come down. They go *out* through body rotation and come *in* as the rotation slows and stops.

If you feel happy about your performance of this first step, then move on to the next. This is to guide your arms into and out of a position, again relying mainly on the momentum provided by rotation although it requires more supervision. We begin with the arms in a state of *inertia*, allow them to gain *momentum* without particularly bothering about their position, but once we become interested in arm position we need *supervision*.

Inertia – Momentum – Supervision

These are the three main factors. Doing the first exercise, only inertia and momentum were needed for the arms, and correct performance was made possible by tension in the lower trunk and legs, and by relaxation in the arms. Now we need the same two factors plus supervision. The supervision is over the position of the arms and shoulders, and involves a conscious balance of tension and relaxation, not simply relaxation. You may appreciate already that the exercises in this chapter call for a much greater awareness of the body state than the awareness we habitually have. When sitting still to do meditation, the body is inactive and relatively easy to focus on. Doing very slow Tai Chi, this focus becomes more difficult. Then in this second exercise it becomes positively dynamic. Much practice is needed.

Turn in a very tight or more open circle, depending on your confidence, using the same alternating V and T steps. V-step toeing in and external T-step toeing out.

1) As you turn and gain momentum, to the right, clockwise, let your arms go up into the basic Pakua position, the Dragon posture, as in figure 8. Do not lift them, just let your arms be raised by the body action, and *supervise* them into this position.

2) Turn three or four revolutions in the same direction and let your body turn keep the momentum swing taking your arms 'ahead' of you to the right.

3) Come to a halt in a V step, and let your arms continue for a second to the right, eventually using your muscles to stop them as you begin revolutions to the left, anticlockwise.

4) Continue in this fashion.

Figure 8 Lifting into Dragon posture

You need a minimum of tension to keep your arm position. Emphasize in your mind the need for relaxation; be aware of relaxation. The tension will take care of itself in the shape the arms take.

Continue to do this exercise over a period of days, regularly, and experience what there is to experience. Then add the following.

1) Repeat the same exercise but as you change from one direction to the other, let the high hand swing down past the abdomen and up into the low hand position: see figures 9 and 10.

2) The tension in the low hand of the first turn, which becomes the high hand in the second, remains more or less constant. The tension in the high hand of the first turn, which becomes

Figures 9 and 10 High hand swinging up

the low hand in the second, alters during the change of direction. As you change, the arm can relax and swing down and up with momentum, needing supervision only in relation to its direction: down and up.

This part of the second exercise shows you how to effect *change* with a minimum of effort. It epitomizes the old Jujutsu and Judo saying: 'maximum result, minimum effort'. A footnote to this is that in the martial arts a relaxed limb travels very much faster than a tensed limb (as when making a punch, for instance). The difficulty for martial artists in this respect is that because they are mainly concerned with fighting, their mental outlook militates against relaxation, in that the generally accepted fighting attitude relies on tension. But that is another story.

Moving on to the third exercise, we want to produce changes *during movement*, again relying on momentum rather than excessive muscle use.

1) Take the position, during rotation, shown earlier in figure 8. Hold this position to the end of several clockwise rotations, then reverse the leg movements.

2) As you do so, let the high hand swing across the front of the body, turning the palm up, as in figure 11, and push the low hand under it, palm up.

3) Continuing to rotate in the same direction, pull the high hand down and let the low hand swing up, out and round, palms vertical, as in figure 12.

Figure 11 Palm up swinging   *Figure 12 Palms vertical*

In time you will realize that this exercise is no more than a specialized version of the Single Palm Change, adapted to suit our purposes. As you develop your ability to do this last exercise using mainly momentum, you will appreciate that the change in position of the arms and hands, during the change of direction in rotation, gives an added momentum to the arms, especially the 'new' high hand – that is, the hand further from the body. The fact that it is pulled in close to the body, as it were left behind, and then has to catch up gives it extra pace when it reaches its new position. You can very readily experiment for yourself using these principles by changing from one Pakua arm position to another.

If we look more closely at the act of turning in one direction and then in another, we find that the moments of change of direction are almost more important than the turning itself. It is hard to quantify but to me it seems that the changeover is crucial. If we focus simply on the leg and foot movements and leave the arms aside for a time, we see that the feet may finish up in a V step or an outward T step position: see figure 13. Furthermore, the weight can be on either leg or evenly distributed. The question is, which do we want, and why?

If the body is rotating to the right, when the feet stop moving the weight will naturally be on the right foot, whether V or T step. The feet stop, the body continues to turn until arrested, and the rotation to the left begins. The left foot leads. It is more convenient and natural, therefore, for the weight to be on the right foot at the end of the right rotation, and on the left foot at the end of the left rotation.

Figure 13 V and outward T step positions

As the feet come to a definite stop, the trunk and arms continue to rotate a little due to momentum. This can be a focus of study – we might consider how much rotation we should allow before arresting it and changing direction. There is surely a straightforward equation, as it were, in which the continued rotation is proportional to the momentum. The continued rotation thus requires supervision. And such supervision will depend also on the fitness of the student.

Such questions are at the heart of Pakua movement in my judgement, and whether the old masters expressed them in quite the same language is not important to us here. What *is* important is that they should be recognized and explored. It is clear to me that in the different Palm Changes the old masters used a variety of arm and trunk positions and movements combined with the leg and feet movements to bring about changes in rotational direction as smoothly as they could. In this respect the central role of the *tantien* or centre of gravity in the lower abdomen can be seen as simply that of a focus of mechanical forces and not as a focus of *chi* or psychological balance. This, however, is a matter of individual preference.

When the body rotates in the fashion described in this chapter, the moment of stopping, followed by the change in direction, reveals the *tantien* as a place of stillness while the upper torso, arms, shoulders and head continue to move momentarily. As the rotation changes direction, the *tantien* is once more a place of focus; and as the rotation takes place, it remains so. This latter point is what Pakua has in common with such other martial arts as Judo and Aikido, Tai Chi and Hsing-I. However much they may differ in alternative respects, they all study *inertia*, *momentum* and *supervision* around the centre of gravity of the lower abdomen. This can be a focus, a firm point, whichever Pakua system you encounter.

Chapter 7

Pakua Chang: Making the Changes

Walking the Circle

Building from the ground up: start with the feet. They can be placed on the ground in three basic ways – the ball of the foot first, the complete sole of the foot as one, and the heel first. Try them, walking in a straight line first, then in a circle of, say, 2 to 2½ metres (6 to 8 feet) in diameter. Just take note of what happens and how your muscles and sense of weight perform. Then do the same thing holding your arms out to the side, slightly bent, as in figure 14.

If you move slowly you can notice the changes in your body and how your muscles adjust to carrying the weight. The same muscles are used, but in a different order.

Method A: the ball of the foot down first
Method B: the whole foot slides forward and down
Method C: the heel down first

Vary Method A by sometimes extending the toes, and sometimes flexing them. Method A can achieve greater forward speed, almost like running. Method B achieves the quickest solidity or firmness. Method C, the most tentative, makes it easier to withdraw the foot to avoid it being swept away by somebody else's leg or foot. I was first taught Method B, and prefer it. Method A can be very tiring, and C is slower. All three methods are used in Pakua, as far as I can ascertain, and indeed some masters at high speed seemed to travel on the rims of their feet, like the blades of ice skates! It will pay you to spend some time on this question of placing the feet. Don't be tempted

Figure 14 Dragon rising from the water posture

to rush on to the more 'interesting' arm movements. Build from the ground up. The reason for walking in straight lines before circling is that it is easier and you are not distracted by keeping to a circle when concentrating on a particular movement or technique.

When you have spent some time following these suggestions, and have made some discoveries for yourself, try something a little different. Look at figure 15. You see two parallel lines connected by two semicircles. Begin walking at point X in a straight line; reaching point Y turn into a curve; reaching point Z resume a straight line; and then turn into a curve again back to the beginning. Try this in both directions. Although nicknamed 'the art of walking the circle', Pakua does use movement in straight lines – especially, it seems, where it has borrowed from

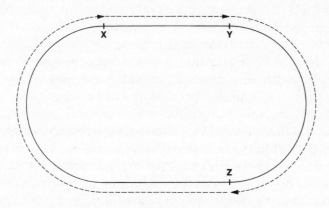

Figure 15 Line and circle combined

the martial art called Hsing-I. Alternating curves and lines will introduce these variations to you at an early stage.

Like other students of Pakua I spent plenty of time walking a circle and varying how I stepped. What I eventually came to like most is a variation of Method B which can be described as 'padding' along. I am thinking of the word as sometimes used to describe a tiger or leopard padding through the jungle. Its etymology is connected with the idea of a *path* and also something *padded*, like a cushion. The foot pads, or gives, as you put it down. It may not suit everyone. Physiques differ, as do temperaments. In Ji Jian Cheng's video programme of the Swimming Dragon Form we see him glide-slide-step each foot forward using Method B. This Form comes directly from Sun Lu Tang. Initially it tells on the abdomen and thighs, but once the effects of exertion are neutralized through training, the effort is well worth it. Or that was my experience when learning from him. When walking, whatever the speed, remember to keep the knee/lower-leg/foot in line. Also, do not let the knee project too much beyond the toes, so putting strain too far forward. If you are new to martial arts, follow this advice because your body may well not have encountered such particular ways of moving before and you could strain joints very easily. Experienced martial artists will know this already.

Once you have tried following figure 15, experiment with circles and lines, devising your own geometrical figures. Perhaps try four steps straight, four steps curved on a big curve; then four straight and four steps curved on a tight curve; and so forth. Relax your upper body and make your abdomen and legs feel firm and strong. The head is erect and the arms held away from the body as if holding two large balls against your sides, but with very little tension. Vary the speed and even the rhythm. Breathe naturally through the nose. If you are observant you will probably come up with questions.

One of these will concern the angles of the feet in relation to the line. Look at figure 16. It shows feet walking in three ways along a curved line. Method 1 shows the feet turned out relative to the line; Method 2 shows the feet following the line; and Method 3 shows feet turned in. All three methods can turn up in Pakua and are not simply experimental. So if your question was about which way to follow, the answer can be to try all

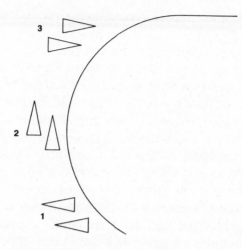

Figure 16 Feet positions relative to circle

three! Once again you can eventually make your own choice. Another question may be about how close the ankles should be as one foot passes the other. Again the answer is: try it. Some practitioners actually brush one ankle against the other as the feet pass.

Then move on to walking a complete circle. Begin with a wide one – say, 2.5 to 3 metres (8 to 10 feet) in diameter or even much bigger. After completing one circuit simply turn around and walk back in the opposite direction. Now keep the steps equidistant and regular in tempo. Up to now you have been doing nothing with the trunk but keeping it relaxed and upright. Now vary this in such a way that if you are walking in a clockwise direction (veering right at all times), you turn your waist to the right – that is, your trunk twists a little towards the centre of the circle. Maintain this for a number of steps then let your trunk relax back to a forward-facing direction. Your abdominal muscles may soon begin to feel it, but with regular training you will get used to it. When you turn your waist the whole trunk, shoulders, and head all turn together. You look towards the imaginary centre of the circle. Reverse direction to vary the muscular effort. The tighter the circle, the more demanding it is on the muscles. If you have plenty of space to train in, go from a very large to a very small circle, just a metre or so (a few feet) across.

Classic Arm Positions

There are several arm positions for walking the circle, each varying a little in details. Some teachers are firm in the details, stressing to pupils that they should conform to them. One of the good reasons for doing what you are told in this direct way is that at least you learn one series of movements correctly according to one teacher. If you then wish to vary the position later, you have a good base from which to start. If you know nothing positively, you have nothing on which to build.

Teachers form their own techniques for several reasons, among which are notions of *chi* flow, martial arts applications, and type of physique and temperament. A good basis from which to adapt if you go to a Pakua class and are asked to change the details of what you do, is shown next. Look at the Dragon position shown in figure 17. The low hand is held away from the body at the elbow. Figures 18 and 19 show variations. In Sun Lu Tang's method the whole of the lower arm is held away from the body. Fingers are apart, palm hollowed to some extent, and there are no prominent knuckles. That is, the fingers extend from the palm and the knuckles do not make a break in the line of the palm and fingers. The index finger of the high hand is either more or less vertical, or, if not vertical, is held higher than the other three. These tend to fall away, lower and lower to the little finger: see figure 20. My own observation and experience indicate that there does not appear to be a rule about this basic palm position, which is sometimes called the Ox Tongue Palm, demonstrated in old photographs of Fu Chen

Figure 17 Dragon position

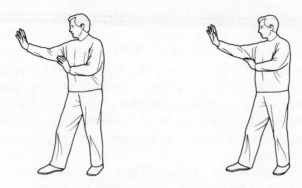

Figures 18 and 19 Variations on Dragon position

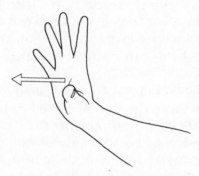

Figure 20 Palm and finger position

Sung and pupils of Kuo Chi-fung. When you are learning from a teacher, you simply follow what he or she says (within reason) and make up your own mind later about what you absorb into your own training.

Try walking in a straight line, turn the waist to the right and begin to place the arm in one of the positions shown above, at right angles to your body. Points to watch are:

- keep the low hand pointing towards, or covering, your high hand elbow;
- keep the low hand elbow away from the body;
- do not make knuckles with either hand.

Swing the arms horizontally to the left, the low hand becoming the high hand, the high hand becoming the low hand. This is just an exercise and not a method of changing the palms. Then switch again to walking the circle. If walking anticlockwise (veering left), the left hand points to the centre and is the high hand. As you walk you can vary the method of placing the feet – toes first, whole foot, heel first, as already described, and also varying the feet to directly follow the line of the circle, or turning slightly out or slightly in. If you pay attention to detail, this series of variations will give you plenty of study, enough for some weeks in fact.

Questions may arise, such as to the position of the shoulder blades. Some teachers say that the shoulder blades should be stretched as taut as a drum skin across the back. Certainly the shoulder blades should not be drawn back towards the spinal column. Another dictum, also open to experiment, is that the *latissimus dorsi* muscles – which run down the sides of the body from the armpits – should be flexed, pulling the shoulders down. But because this can restrict breathing, it should not be done continuously.

Other questions that may arise are related to the purpose of the three foot positions: turned in, turned out, or kept in line. The reasons for them depend on what they are preparing you to do. Turning out prepares you for performing any technique in which you turn away from the centre of the circle. Stepping in line with the circle prepares you for making further movements along this line. And turning in prepares you for turning into the circle as you make variations in arm and body movement.

If you spend time reflecting in this way while you are training, you will understand what you are doing much better than if you simply do what you are told like a robot! Your thinking will inform your movement and give it better form, a sense of purpose. You will begin to think about the purpose of movement, about what in Karate is called *bunkai*: the application of technique from a *kata*.

This book is not about any particular style of Pakua but a general introduction which I believe will give you a good grounding. Think of the centre of the circle as an opponent, or if not an opponent, a focus. You keep the focus in focus. Try all the above in small, middle, and large circles, clockwise and anticlockwise. Then move on to the next stage.

Making Changes in Direction

Pakua Chang is to do with changing, making changes, as inspired by the *I Ching*, the Book of Changes. Basic to the art are eight Palm Changes. There is variation in style here too, but variety can be interesting. This book presents one variation based on the changes used in modern *Wushu* training programmes. In fact it seems to have been based on the Old Fu Style of Fu Chen Sung, a second-generation teacher. For one thing it uses more steps over which the changes can be made where other styles use fewer steps or even body spinning. This is a good thing from the point of view of beginners because they will have more training in placing the feet correctly and will be able to experiment for themselves when trying out the V step and T step. (The animal names are printed under many of the illustrations.)

FIRST CHANGE

The first Palm Change teaches how to turn in, towards the centre of the circle; then out, away from the centre; then in again, to face and walk in the opposite direction. So if you were walking clockwise, veering right, right high hand, you would turn in rightward until you turned out from the circle and began moving anticlockwise, left high hand.

1) Walk the circle clockwise: figure 21.

Figure 21 Black Dragon turns its head right

2) When the right foot is in front, bring the left foot forward and round to make a V step, figure 22, turning the whole body, as one, to your right.

3) Keep the momentum of the turn going by turning the right foot out and taking a short step, figure 23, the whole body moving as one, and turn the right palm horizontally away from you. Keep your eyes on the right hand.

4) Keep the momentum of the turn going. Bring the left foot round to make a V step with the right: figure 24. At the same time thrust the left palm under the right armpit keeping it away from the body, not touching it. The thrust of the left palm is done with a twisting action of the whole arm and the turning of the palm upwards towards the underside of the right upper arm.

Figure 22 V step

Figure 23 T step

Figure 24 Black Dragon turns left

Figure 25 Turning left

5) Begin to turn the whole body to the left, figure 25. Twist the little finger edge of the right palm inwards towards the centre of the body, and simultaneously curve the left palm upwards from the right to the left of the body past the triceps muscles and the elbow of the right arm.

6) Continue to turn to your left, back towards the centre of the circle. Raise the left hand higher, keeping the right palm close to the inside edge of the left upper arm, and begin to twist the little finger edges of both hands away from the body: figure 26. As this happens, begin to lower your palms until you find yourself in the position in figure 27. The left foot steps out along the circle line as you lower your palms into position.

Students of Tai Chi may compare this movement with the Yang-style movement of Fair Lady Works With Shuttle to appreciate a similarity between it and the movement of the Single Palm Change (our first Palm Change). There are other similarities, but I leave them for readers to discover.

Some points to watch in the first Palm Change movement are:

- Use the waist action and stepping action of the feet together; do not separate them.

- Keep the right elbow down as the palm goes horizontal.

- Twist both arms strongly inwards as you turn back to the left.

- Do not make knuckles as you move your palms.

Figure 26 Continuing to turn left   *Figure 27 Step into anti-clockwise walking*

Explore and try out the first Palm Change many times, as if at a teacher's insistence. Search for coordination. Observe that you make a twisting action of the body to the left (or right) initially, and try to work out what is the best way to initiate the returning movement back in the opposite direction. Do you twist keeping the abdomen/navel at exactly the same height, and the ribcage at the same height? Or do you rotate them slightly down, up, and round, lifting the ribcage a little at the same time? What part do the thighs and knees play? Try it and see what works for you.

There are two further pointers before moving on to the Double Palm Change. The first is a variation on stepping, now that you are more skilled. Using Method B, try putting your leading foot down 'empty', that is with no weight on it, and then send it forward a further 20 to 30 centimetres (8 to 12 inches) before transferring weight on to it. This method eventually gives more speed and distance, and is therefore useful for evasion and distance closing. The second pointer is to bring the knees inwards, slightly, when stepping and when making the V step.

SPINNING

The above points all add up to making the first Palm Change accessible. When you feel comfortable with that method you can introduce spinning. Instead of making the first V step to face into the circle, if walking clockwise, step out with the right foot, and as you bring the left foot round spin on the right foot through 270 degrees, three-quarters of a circle. This will bring you out facing in the opposite direction *and* facing away

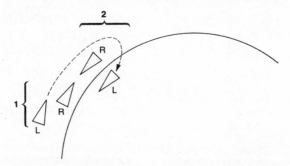

Figure 28 Spinning to change direction

from the centre of the circle. Thread the arms in the same way as you did when doing the V steps, but more rapidly and in synchronization with your spin. Then step out and back along the line of the circle with your left foot in an anticlockwise direction.

This spinning action is a preparation for the final method. Walking clockwise again, step out with the right foot, spin on it, and bring the left foot round in a 'hairpin' shape and step out straight along the circle's curve: see figure 28.

SECOND CHANGE

The second change – the Double Palm Change – begins and ends like the Single Palm Change, but extra movements are sandwiched between. Return to the first method of stepping as if about to do the first change, walking anticlockwise and veering left, left high hand pointing towards the centre. Make the first V step towards the centre, then step out with the left foot and make the second V step away from the centre. So far these are the first Palm Change movements. Next, take the left foot a few inches behind you so that the toes rest close to your right heel, and the heel of the left foot is slightly raised: figure 29. As you make this step, twist a little to the left, quickly driving the right palm high and the left palm low down to the right knee. Then spin to the left and, with the weight on the right foot, step into a type of horse riding stance, sweeping the left hand above the left knee and the right hand down to the right knee: see figure 30. Carry on thereafter into the final phases of the first

Figure 29 Hawk soars into the sky

Figure 30. White Snake hides in the grass

Palm Change. Turn out with the left foot, V-step with the right foot, arms threading as before, and step out with the right foot to walk the circle again.

At first do the foot movements as steps. When you are clear about the changes in direction and arrive in the correct places, you can introduce spinning. Points to watch are:

- Drive the right hand high and left low with twisting strength, but approach this unusual movement cautiously until your muscles are used to it.

- As you make the heel raised stance with the left foot, begin a spin or turn which carries right through until you are in the V step and coming out of your Double Palm Change.

- Apart from their exercise value, these spinning movements and powerful, fluid twists and turns represent effective and unusual martial arts techniques, so think of yourself sometimes as if under attack from punches, kicks, and grappling techniques.

THIRD CHANGE

Personally, I found the third Palm Change very appealing when I first encountered it, perhaps because of the complete and immediate change of direction from facing inward to facing outward. The way the palms are used in this example from the Wushu syllabus is different from Sun Lu Tang style, for instance, but the method and direction of turn is similar.

Walking in a clockwise direction (veering right, right high hand), take a step with the left foot away from the centre of the circle. As you make this step bend the right arm back towards the head so that the forearm is a few inches from, and slightly above, your forehead. At the same time look left, as in figure 31. The left palm stays facing the same direction as before relative to the trunk – that is, reaching across the front of it. The torso twists to the left. To emphasize that several things happen at once in all Pakua techniques, here is a list of all of them for this first movement:

- step out with the left foot away from the circle

Figure 31 Snake turns darting out its tongue

- begin to twist the torso to the left

- look left outwards away from the centre

- keep the left arm-palm pointing across the front of the body, not touching it

- remember that this is the beginning of what will become a continuous spinning movement

Make a V step with the right foot, turning the left palm to face down, and bringing the right palm facing down to it so that both arms cross in front of the trunk: see figure 32. Continue your anticlockwise twist to the left, bringing the left palm and right palm to the left and right knees respectively with a sweeping action, not touching the knees. This arm movement is

Figure 32 Dragon draws back its tail

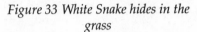

Figure 33 White Snake hides in the   *Figure 34 Beginning Black Dragon*
grass   *turns*

accompanied by a step to your left with your left foot, into a horse riding stance, as in figure 33. Keep your gaze on the left knee and hand region.

Turn out with the left foot, and as you do so make a big step round with your right foot to make a V step, driving the right palm up and under the left armpit with the palm-facing-upward twist, and turn the left palm upwards also, as in figure 34. Turn towards the right, raising the arms as though finishing off the Single Palm Change, and step out along the circle. Points to watch are:

- Keep the elbows away from body.

- Aim to make your steps into swivels as you V step – that is, the supporting leg steps and turns as the other leg makes the V shape.

- The head always follows the direction of movement.

FOURTH CHANGE

The fourth Palm Change begins a more complex series of movements. It is tough to exercise discipline when going into something new in the martial arts, but if you can, try to be clear in outline, at least, about the first three Changes before moving on to the fourth. Moving on too fast to such complicated moves, you might become confused, waste time, and be discouraged. Then you might have to start all over again.

Begin walking the circle with the right hand high, and make a V step with the left foot turning into the centre. You are turning right, so continue to turn right, stepping out with the right foot away from the centre. As your right foot makes the turn, turn your right palm to its right – that is, lower the thumb edge and raise the little finger edge, as in figure 35. Keep the left palm vertical, guarding the right elbow and ribcage. Next, step along the line of the circle with the left foot, and at the same time turn the little finger edge of the right palm downwards, rotating the palm over to your left side and then drawing it back to your left shoulder, as in figure 36. Synchronizing with this right arm movement, push out the left palm and twist it under your right upper arm, palm up. When you reach this stage of the Change your right palm is down and the left palm up.

To clarify what I mean I will go through this movement again in different words. Turn the little finger edge of the right palm down in a small scooping action and sweep across the front of your body in a horizontal plane. The shape it makes is the arc of a circle. As the palm makes this arc is should be facing up, but then turn it to face down and pull it in nearer the left shoulder.

Make a V step by turning on the left foot, drawing the right elbow down, as in figure 37. Thrust out with the right palm, raising the right knee, as in figures 38 and 39. Spin to the right, stepping out with the right foot, sweeping horizontally round

Figures 35 and 36 Swallow flies into the forest

Figures 37 and 38 Black Dragon stretches out its claw (i)

Figure 39 Black Dragon stretches   *Figure 40 Monkey moves the*
out its claw (ii)   *branches*

with the right hand in a slight dipping curve, and bring the left
hand round the body to finish opposite the left lower ribs, as in
figure 40. Bring the left foot round in a V step, twining the arms
as at the end of the Single Palm Change, and complete the move
as in the Single Palm Change, left hand high. Points to watch
are:

• Keep rotating or twisting or twining the arms like a coiling
  snake.

• When you bring the elbow down, do not let it touch the body.

• The eyes and head move with the direction, the leading
  edge.

FIFTH CHANGE

The fifth Palm Change is longer still. Walk clockwise with right hand high. Turn the left foot in to make a V step as in the Single Palm Change in figure 41. Take a step along the circle line, with the right foot pushing ahead with the right palm. At the same time draw the left palm back, palm up, to the left hip bone, but not touching it. Then draw back the right palm, rotating and in an arc as in the fourth Change, and thrust the left palm out and under the right upper arm as you do this, finishing with palm up, as in figure 42. Swivel right on both feet, and push the left hand high behind you, and the right in front of your solar plexus, as in figure 43. Take a deep step back with the right foot and thrust the left palm forwards in front of your forehead, palm away from you, thumb edge down. As the left palm does

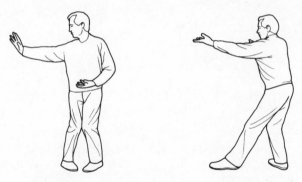

Figures 41 and 42 Swallow flies into the forest

Figure 43 Horse turns its head (i) (two views)

Figure 44 Horse turns its head (ii)

Figures 45 and 46 White Monkey offers up fruit

this, push down with the right palm past the ribs and right hip to the thigh, as in figure 44. The right palm faces up to finish. Then spin on the left foot and sweep the right leg to the right, as in figure 45. As you do so, push the right palm forward, twisting it to face downwards, and push the left palm, facing upwards, to be level with the left waist. Make a big step with the left foot to form a V step as in the ending to the Single Palm Change, crossing the arms at the elbow but not touching them together. Turn left and step out with the left foot, bringing the left arm around to the front of the chest, and draw both elbows close in to one another and maybe 15 centimetres (6 inches) away from the body, as in figure 46. The palms should be turned outwards, as shown. Walk the circle in this position, sometimes called Monkey Offers Up Fruit. Points to watch are:

- Demands are made on the legs in this Change, with its deep steps. To begin with take small steps with high stances to get used to it.

- Keep the elbows down.

- Keep the turns continuous once you feel confident about directions and degrees of turning.

SIXTH CHANGE

The sixth Palm Change starts from a different arm position. To reach it, start from the Holding-a-ball position, as shown in figure 47. Step out with the left foot to walk the circle anticlockwise, and as you step, push out the hands simultaneously. The right arm rises past the right side of the face to reach a point away from, and above, your right temple; and the left pushes palm-up to 'point' to the centre of the circle, as in figure 48. As you take the initial step turn the waist inwards towards the centre.

After a few steps make a V step with the right foot to join the left, which turns inwards towards the centre, as in figure 49. Then immediately turn out away from the centre with the left foot, and make another V step with the right foot. The arms maintain their Holding-a-ball high pose. Take a step left with the left foot, bringing the left palm inwards in a downward-moving curve, palm down, past the solar plexus and keeping your right palm equidistant from it so that they move in unison,

Figures 47 and 48 Lion holds a ball (i)

Figures 49 and 50 Lion holds a ball (ii)

Figures 51 and 52 Lion holds a ball (iii)

maintaining their shape, as if cradling or holding a ball. The upper torso and arms move as one: see figure 50.

Step forward with the right foot and continue to sweep your left palm down past your groin and up in front of your left side, palm down, while the right palm sweeps past your knees and into a continued and maintained Holding-a-ball position, as in figure 51. V step. Think of this movement as rolling a ball from above your head-left-side, across your body and down in front of your right side, across your body and up in front of your left side. Step back with the left foot, swivelling on the right foot, carrying the ball down your left side by lowering the left hand a little and raising the right, as in figure 52. Roll the ball across the knees to the right so that you are holding it above your knees, and step back behind you through 180 degrees with your left foot, as in figure 53.

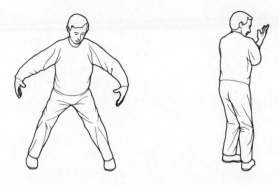

Figures 53 and 54 Lion holds a ball (iv)

Figures 55 and 56 Lion holds a ball (v)

Swivel on the left foot and make a V step by bringing the right foot to it, twisting and pushing the right palm under the left armpit region, both palms facing up, as in figure 54. Turn right and step out right, turning from the waist right and pushing the left palm up and over the head, palm down, and bringing the right arm round with the turn of the waist to thrust out, palm up, in the Holding-a-ball position again, as in figures 55 and 56. Make a V step by bringing the left foot round to the right. Step right with the right foot and repeat the exercise of rolling the ball around the body but using opposite arms and legs. Figures 57–60 give an idea of the approximate movement of the 'ball'.

Obviously the move can be repeated as many times as you wish, walking in either direction. Points to watch are:

*Figure 57 Lion rolls a ball –
beginning to 'roll' (i)*

*Figure 58 Lion rolls a ball –
continuing to roll (ii)*

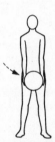

*Figure 59 Lion rolls a ball –
continuing to roll (iii)*

*Figure 60 Lion rolls a ball –
completing roll on opposite
side of body (iv)*

- This move is sometimes called Lion Holds (or Plays With or Rolls) a Ball. Keep this idea in mind as you train, to familiarize yourself with it. The ball is held and rotated in time with the turning of the body and the steps.

- Keep the arms bent and *feel* them being curved (of course they do not actually curve although you can sometimes have the impression that they really do).

SEVENTH CHANGE

The seventh Palm Change introduces kicking and crossing the legs. It is longer and more complex, so be careful not to rush through the instructions and leave gaps in your learning: fill in all the gaps before you continue. Keep notes if you are not sure.

Mark a circle on the ground if facilities exist, and mark the foot placements in chalk. When I am doing and teaching Tai Chi and Pakua myself, I have a wooden floor which takes chalk marks that can easily be rubbed out without making permanent impressions on the wood. You may not need it, but sometimes to have to draw out the changes yourself, and to mark the 'orbits' of the arms, can throw new light on the subject for the teacher as well as for the pupils.

For the seventh change, begin walking clockwise, right arm high in the same posture as for the Single Palm Change. When the left foot is ahead, turn the right palm up and 'cut' to the left with it, at the same time drawing the left palm, facing up, back to the left hip. This is an inward chopping, slicing or cutting action with the right palm, as in figure 61. As you move the arms, bring the right foot up, toes level with the left heel, and keep the heel of the right foot just off the ground. The next move should be a smooth and continuous follow-up to the previous one, as will be clear when you can do it. Turn right, stepping back with the right foot in the direction from which you came. As you make this swivelling return, continue the slicing action of the right hand by turning the palm down and cutting horizontally to the right, with a slight downward and upward dip and rise, as in figure 62. The left hand stays in place. You can now see that the first cut from right to left then curves into the second cut from left to right, combined with a change in palm position, from facing up to facing down.

Now, using your right heel as a pivot, turn the right foot out to the right and bring the left knee close in behind the right

Figures 61 and 62 Waving Fan in front of the gate

knee joint to form a cross-legged sort of stance, as in figure 63. Combine the foot movement with that of the arms by sliding the left palm under the right forearm then out to the left to form a posture similar to Monkey Offers Up Fruit. Both palms face upwards. The trunk is turned to the right, and you look at the right palm. The turn continues to the right as you bring the left foot round to make a V step, the hands remaining in place, as in figure 64. Then separate the palms widely to the sides and kick up high with the right heel: see figures 65a and b.

Step downwards with the right foot to the back, driving the right hand, palm up, over the head and to the left side of the head, and pull the left palm, facing up, to the left hip, as in figure 66. The weight is mainly on the left leg at this point. Then swing the right hand strongly down towards the inside of your right lower leg, palm down, and 'squat' on the left leg, as in figure 67. The left hand stays in place. Turn the right foot out

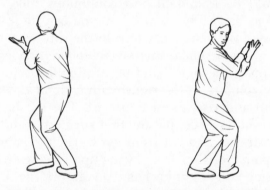

Figures 63 and 64 Phoenix spreads its wings (i)

Figures 65a and b Phoenix spreads its wings (ii)

Figures 66 and 67 Swallow flies over the water

Figures 68a and b Windmill (i)

and bring the left foot round in a big, quick movement, to make a V step, at the same time thrusting round, clockwise with the left palm, facing up, and bring the right palm, facing downwards, and strike horizontally to the right with the point of the elbow, as in figures 68a and b.

Bring the left palm round, facing up, just below the right elbow. And as you complete the elbow strike, pull the body weight back on to the left leg even more, and, making a fist with the left hand, palm down, make a back fist strike with the right hand, as in figure 69. Turn right again, bringing the left foot round to make a V step, and thrust the left palm under the right armpit with both palms facing up, as in the close of the Single Palm Change: figure 70. Turn left, and step out left, bringing the arms momentarily into the Monkey Offers Up Fruit position, as

Figure 69 Windmill (ii)

Figure 70 Threading the arms

Figures 71 and 72 Dragon rises from the water

in figure 71, and then continue to push the palms out into the final position, shown in figure 72.

Points to watch are:

- Ensure that the first and second moves are continuous, two cuts in one.

- Tuck the left knee in close to the back of the right knee joint.

- By this time your training should have led you to be able to move with continuity, like a swimming fish.

- Make your attacking movements strong, fast, and momentarily focused.

EIGHTH CHANGE

The final, eighth Palm Change includes much of what you have already done, with additions. Walk in the first position, clockwise (veering right), right hand high. From a position in which the right foot is ahead, swing your right arm and palm to the left, and push the left palm under the right armpit as you make a left foot step, as in figure 73. Follow the movement of the right arm with your eyes and head. Continue to swing your right palm to the left, bending the elbow even more, and follow its movement with your eyes and head, stepping with the right foot, as in figure 74. Turn your body to the right as you shift weight on to the right foot, and turn the right palm to face

Figure 73 and 74 Fling the sleeves into the wind (i)

Figures 75 and 76 Fling the sleeves into the wind (ii)

Figures 77 and 78 Fling the sleeves into the wind (iii)

Figure 79 Fling the sleeves into the wind (iv)

Figure 80 Monkey steps on a branch

Figure 81 Swallow flies over the water

Figure 82 Snake turns over (i)

upwards and bring the right elbow above the left wrist, as in figure 75. Step forward with the right foot, and strike forward and up with the upward-facing palm, as in figure 76.

You will see that the last three moves are really one continuous block-block-stroke action. As you do the moves shown in figures 77 and 78, lean slightly backwards as though avoiding or deflecting a couple of blows. Then, as in figure 79, move your body forwards as you thrust upwards and forwards.

Raise the right knee and kick upwards with the toe, as in figure 80. Swing the right foot backwards and swivel right, sweeping the right hand down in a slicing movement, palm down, and drawing the left palm back to the left hip, palm up, as in figure 81. Crouch low as you make this movement, then straighten up, stepping forward with the left foot and thrusting horizontally with the left palm face-up. Cover the left upper arm with the right palm face-down, as in figure 82.

Make a very rapid V step with the left foot to the right foot, and turn the torso right, at the same time twisting the left palm clockwise, palm up, bringing the right palm above your left temple, palm facing away from the face as though defending your head, as in figure 83. With a strong action raise the right knee and thrust forward with the right palm face-upwards, lifting the left arm to give added force, as in figure 84.

Step backwards with the right foot, swivelling to your right with the left foot, and slice horizontally with a slight downward dip with the right palm, turning the palm downwards. At the same time bring the left palm round to the left hip, palm down,

Figures 83 and 84 Snake turns over (ii)

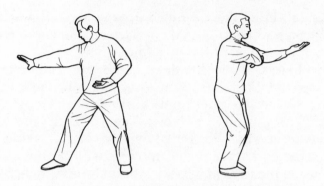

Figures 85 and 86 Swallow flies into the forest

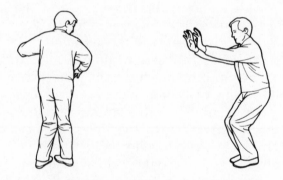

Figures 87a and b Tiger springs on its prey

as in figure 85. Turn out with the right foot through 180 degrees, as in figure 86, thrusting the left palm, face-up, under the right upper arm, and pulling the right palm back to cover the left upper arm. Continue to turn right on the left foot by stepping behind you through 180 degrees, and bring the left foot next to the right, left heel raised, as in figure 87a. As you do so, bring both palms out to the sides, elbows bent, as though holding a tray in each palm, then push both palms simultaneously forwards past the ears and strike horizontally forwards with both palms: see figure 87b.

Turn with a right foot swivel into a V step, bringing the left foot to the right, and cross both arms as in the conclusion of the Single Palm Change. Raise the arms left, and turn left, as in the

Single Palm Change, and step out left with the arms in the first basic Walking the Circle position. Points to watch are:

- Keep elbows down as before.

- Follow the leading hand with the eyes and head.

- Regulate your turns so that you do not spin too far or too little and end up in the wrong position for resuming your walking of the circle.

- If you do end up in the wrong position, practise making a much larger or smaller final movement to bring yourself into the right alignment with the circle. This will involve a spinning movement to make up distance or a tiny turn if you have travelled too far.

This concludes, in outline, the movements of the eight Changes. If you follow the pictures and words you will come to a fair enough performance of them. Any previous experience of the martial arts should be of help. Above all, be patient, observant, and intelligent!

Chapter 8

The Essential Ingredient

If you take a piece of string and tie a knot in it, leave a space, tie a second knot, leave a space, and tie a third knot, you end up with an arrangement like the one in figure 88. This represents a linear approach to a subject: in this case, Pakua. The first knot can stand for correct stepping, the second knot for correct arm position, and the third knot for correct placing of the head. Another example could be a situation of medical emergency. A woman cuts herself badly. The first knot can stand for stopping the bleeding, the second for applying a pad and fixing it in place, and the third for treatment for shock.

Both these sequences of measures are, on the face of it, sound ones. But they both have important limitations. In the Pakua example, experience shows that none of the three requirements – stepping, arm position, head position – can be achieved correctly if dealt with in isolation, using such a linear approach: first this, then this, then this. The reason for the difficulty is that if you correct one thing at a time, in a living, moving organism, other things may go wrong. Clearly there are exceptions to this generalization, as in the medical example cited. But for instance in Pakua, if you leave point number one and go on to point number two, point number one may go wrong because you have stopped paying attention to it. It is a usual function of the human central nervous system that as soon as you cease giving extra attention to a process to modify it, the former behaviour returns.

Moving back to the medical example, the linear approach is possible in this instance because the problem is simple. If the woman displays no more symptoms than bleeding and mild shock, she is quite safe. But suppose she has been cut in several

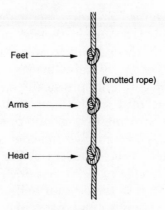

Feet ───▶
(knotted rope)
Arms ───▶
Head ───▶

Figure 88 Linear approach

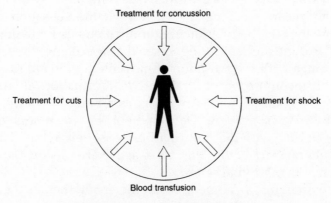

Treatment for concussion

Treatment for cuts   Treatment for shock

Blood transfusion

Figure 89 Simultaneous approach

places at once, say by flying glass; that her blood clotting mechanism is not functioning as well as it might; that she goes into severe shock; that she has also hit her head and is suffering from concussion. What she needs is simultaneous medical care on many fronts, as indicated by figure 89. This diagram shows a combination of measures, a combination of linear approaches, all taking place simultaneously:

- stopping bleeding in several places

- assistance with clotting

- treatment for shock

- surveillance for the effects of concussion.

This needs, say, three or four medically trained people. Together their combined ability, their combined brains form one brain, as it were, focused on treating the injured woman. One brain, one person, might know everything that needs to be done, but one person could not physically do it.

The farcical image of a similar approach to Pakua training shows that the medical method is not practical. One teacher corrects the head, while another teacher corrects the arms, while another teacher corrects the feet, while another teacher . . . Farcical or not, the image is a graphic one and shows that the Pakua student has to find the several helpers inside himself or herself. Then the question is, how is this to be brought about?

It can be brought about through the development of vigilance and awareness. Vigilance means watching, and awareness in this case means keeping in touch with the sensation of the movement of the body. Watching in turn entails knowing what has to be done and observing to see that it is being done. Keeping in touch with the sensation of movement is an aid to watching. The incoming or proprioceptive information about how your body is moving already exists as a natural faculty of the central nervous system. Development of awareness means getting in tune with that information, those sensations. This is a fundamental part of the *internal* martial arts, using the word *internal* in its most vital sense.

Digressing for a moment from the main theme, there are occasions when a person can see a new set of movements being performed and copy them exactly. As I write, I picture a young woman, a dancer, who is learning Tai Chi from me. During the first two lessons she saw and copied about eight of the opening movements of the Yang-style Short Form perfectly. The existing class members watched in amazement. You could say that on the face of it she did not need to develop her awareness. What we beheld was an example of someone doing something and not interfering with the process. Unfortunately for our current argument, she began to make mistakes before the second lesson was over, and could not 'recapture that first fine careless rapture'! She unconsciously lost contact with her immaculate copying talent, and had to begin to think what was wrong and what had to be done. She was also very tired and had used up her attention. She became impatient with herself and a little fretful. She had to begin the 'several helpers' approach.

People who have studied Tai Chi or meditation or some such discipline well, know the experience of a change in the substance of the body. It is hard to describe. It may be a sensation of lightness, or weight, or clarity; any number of subjective descriptions can be applied. Part of this new experience consists of becoming in tune with processes in the body-mind system from which we are normally cut off. We recognize this new experience as a welcome and desirable one. It is produced, to some extent, by the combination of vigilance and awareness mentioned above. During this experience, awareness is spread out – it is not locked in to one thought, one emotion, one physical movement. It is like looking at a country scene and taking it all in at once, instead of admiring one flower or one tree.

Turning to Pakua training, for example, the goal of total awareness would point to the need for connectedness in movement: 'The whole body moves as one unit', as the classics say. Even if you perform a movement incorrectly, it is better to do it and be aware of as much of the body as possible than to get it right and not be very much aware of anything. Awareness is literally central to Walking Meditation. A similar approach is found in the many therapies around today. It is axiomatic that you should *listen* to a patient or client, and not *tell* him or her. We all know how people who are always handing out advice turn us off – but a good listener receives a much better reception. The persistent adviser is a linear worker, if that is the word, whereas the listener is a simultaneous worker. So as the patient speaks and becomes more confident and trusting, the real problems may come to the surface. Likewise with moving the body: as the awareness listens to the movement and the vigilance watches, gradually the intelligence of moving can appear. It is no longer a question of do this, then do that, then do the other. Furthermore, this approach shows that we are all different, up to a point. One person will take longer than another; one person will reach better awareness in one way, and another person in another way.

PRACTICAL

The following exercise is one that I use in my own teaching. It has appeared in another of my books but I make no excuse for using it again. It can be a starting-point for the development of vigilance and awareness in movement.

1) Stand in a normal upright position, feet together, arms by the sides. Let go.

2) Raise the right foot and place the back edge of the heel of that foot directly ahead of you, in line with the right hip joint. Using the muscle on the outer edge of your shin, pull the foot gently towards you as you place the heel down. Only the heel of the foot touches the floor.

3) Simultaneously bend the left knee sufficiently to allow the sole of the right foot to touch the floor and lower the right sole to the floor. Do not put any weight on the right foot, and relax the hip joint, knee joint and ankle joint of the right foot.

4) Shift your weight on to the right foot, bending the right knee a little, and raise the heel of the left foot so that the foot is resting on the ball of the foot. Allow the left knee to bend naturally.

5) Do the same with the left foot.

There are more movements to this exercise, but the above is the basic. It is simple, easy to remember, but very effective and interesting when combined with *vigilance, awareness* and *relaxation*. It is perhaps best done when you have already exercised enough to be warmed up but are breathing normally. In Step 1 wait in a standing position until you are focused and are aware of your body, standing, waiting. In Step 2 do not allow yourself to put any more weight on your right heel than the weight which the leg itself has. In Step 3 be sure to bend the left knee and lower the right sole at the same time; you must still let no weight move on to the right foot than the weight that the leg itself has; relax all your right leg. In Step 4 move your weight firmly forward with no hesitation, and simultaneously raise the left heel.

Perform this simple sequence of movement until you can do it with no mistakes whatsoever. If you find that you keep shifting your weight on to the right leg prematurely, you are not ready for the next phase. Restraining the weight shift is most important. Shifting the weight immediately is what you usually do when walking – you don't want that. This is an error that constantly creeps in during the first phase.

Once the first phase is clear, begin to relax your body as you move. Taking one obvious area at a time, relax it as you walk. But when you stop focusing on relaxing your buttocks, for instance, and begin to relax your abdomen or chest, continue to keep some awareness reserved for relaxing your buttocks. Carry on like this until you are able to be aware of the whole of your relaxed body.

The vigilance, awareness and relaxation needed in this exercise is enough to last anyone a lifetime.

Chapter 9

Taoist Philosophy

The Taoist schools of Chinese philosophy and training are said to have been originated by people who studied history and who therefore reflected on successes and failures, rises and falls, in the affairs of men. By pursuing these studies they perceived the essentials, and proceeded through life with meekness and purity. This at least is the theory of Liu Hsin, writing at the beginning of the Christian era. The Taoist schools became an established part of Chinese beliefs. It was only later that other philosophers began to unite Yin-Yang philosophy with Taoist philosophy. This is worth pointing out because there is a widespread belief among Westerners that Yin-Yang philosophy began with the Taoist school. Liu Hsin maintained that Yin-Yang philosophy came from the official astronomers. As time passed, more and more different schools appeared and were sometimes referred to as 'the hundred schools', meaning very many. Teachings, ideas, and sometimes mere slivers of thought crossed from one school to another. However, my research has failed to find any specific origin of the Taoists – neither I nor anyone else knows who brought the word *tao* into use for the first time in a philosophical context, or what his antecedents were. Taoism simply 'originated'.

In the *Analects of Confucius* we read that during the period when Confucius (born 551 BC) travelled extensively from one state of China to another, he met men who were called *yin che*, meaning 'those who obscure themselves'. These men regarded Confucius with some disdain, saying that he knew that he could not succeed in reforming society, but that nevertheless he went on trying. He was beating his head against a brick wall. In spite of this opinion, many people of course see Confucius as an important and valuable contributor to Chinese culture. The eminent historian Fung Yu Lan wrote in his *Short History of Chinese Philosophy* that 'it was from men of this sort [*yin che*], most of them living far away from other men in the world of nature, that the Taoists were *probably* drawn.'

The best known early Taoist was Yang Chu, who lived around 380 BC. His teaching was that one should live without becoming entangled in the affairs of life. One should preserve what is genuine. This theme of being able to maintain a kind of distance between oneself and the phenomena of life, both outside and inside oneself, is constant in this period of early Taoism. But the method, training or inner efforts necessary to achieve this relationship are not, to my knowledge, explained in the writings of the time. The literature I have encountered explains what the relationship produces, but not how. In the *Yellow Emperor's Classic of Internal Medicine* or *Nei Ching Su Wen*, we find references to the sages of old, and how they could pre-serve the essence, be tranquil, and harmonize with the changes in life. They restrained their desires and found satisfaction in simplicity, each living for a long time. But again, *how* they did so is not clear. A related suggestion, popularized in the press recently, is that eating only a little, but in a balanced way, can increase longevity. It has been found to work in experimental animals.

The implication is of course that the means existed, or else the writings would be based merely on empty words, wishful thinking. Fung Yu Lan refers to the writings of later Taoists such as Lao-tzu and Chuang-tzu who were influenced by Yang Chu. In one book, the *Lu-shih Ch'un-ch'iu* by Chuang-tzu, there is a chapter entitled 'The Importance of Self' in which the fact of having a life, of being born, is extolled as more important than becoming Emperor, gaining the whole world, and so on. It is reminiscent of the Christian saying about gaining the whole world and losing one's soul. Commentators on the early Taoist view have said that they despised the world. Others have described them as nihilists, cynics, and so forth. My own under-standing of this is that 'despising' does not accurately represent the Taoist attitude to the world of men. It is too petty, too small an attitude for such a great school of philosophy. The book *Tao Te Ching* attributed to Lao-tzu displays an attitude to or understanding of the world that has nothing to do with despising it. It is closer to the idea expressed by GI Gurdjieff of not being 'identified' with the world, with emotions and with thoughts.

It seems clear, then, that a means of developing a different inner attitude to life existed in these early days, and that one of its main features was the capacity to keep what is genuine and valuable in one's being from becoming caught up in the daily travails of ordinary life. In Lao-tzu's works there is a development of this approach in relation to the universe and the social and political lives of men. Chuang-tzu put it very well: 'using things as things, but not being used by things as things.'

As Taoism grew in influence in China, so did the Yin-Yang school of philosophy, and the teachings on the Five Elements. The latter are primal 'substances' from which everything else is made, as well as being phases through which processes pass. Tung Chung-chu, who lived around 104 BC, brought the Five Elements and the Yin-Yang philosophy together. The *I Ching* also exerted its own influence at this period, of course, so it is difficult for a modern student to appreciate what a multiplicity of ideas and teachings then faced a prospective student all those centuries ago.

In the legends, stories and histories of the martial arts, we read how martial artists, who later become famous, meet a recluse, a hermit, a Taoist and learn from him some secret method. The fruits of this method appear to the outside world as a new martial arts system or style. If only a small fraction of the stories are true, we have to assume that a Taoist method which influenced martial artists existed for at least 2,500 years, and was passed down through the generations to the present day. Yin Shih Tzu is an example of someone who embodied the teaching, and who proclaimed himself. But for one Taoist who did this there must have been many more who did not. Can we assume that these secret Taoists understood even more than the ones who became well known? It is likely.

Similarly, we read again, especially in the cases of less recent martial artists, that they often accepted few students, and of these taught only selected students their 'inner secrets'. Where a teacher accepted many students, he would take just a few and teach them the whole system. So however many learned something, there were very few who learned everything. We can thus, conclude that for this reason the numbers of full initiates always remained low. This conclusion says something about the lifestyle and training mentioned earlier. Was the lifestyle particularly difficult? Did the training require the close personal attention of the teacher? Were only a few people suitable? All these questions suggest that only a small, limited number of initiates was *possible*.

This conclusion, if true, may be connected with a practice of the Taoists which we in the West call alchemy. It is popularly regarded as a means of changing lead or base metals into gold – but it is no secret that this is simply an analogy: the 'base metals' represent ordinary human nature and the 'gold' refers to the ideal form that a human can attain. The fire that transforms the base metal is the fire of inner effort, inner work. What is less well known is the idea, also put forward by Gurdjieff, that there is a limited amount of gold – that not everyone can find gold. Once again one can hardly refrain from thinking of the Christian saying that 'many are called but few are chosen'. This would explain also the fact that a teacher took on very few 'inner-chamber' students. He had limited time and limited resources, and could not waste either on unsuitable people.

The next question that arises is what such teachers were teaching to their inner students. Do we know? The answer is Yes, for we have explanations, diagrams and accounts of personal experiences. Consult any book on Yoga meditation, Buddhist meditation, Tibetan meditation, Taoist meditation, and anything derived from these, and you will find diagrams of energy pathways through the human body. Although they may differ in detail, they all show channels or paths travelling up and down the body. The methods of conducting the energy along the channels are learned from an experienced teacher. What martial artists have tried to do is to employ these methods, or similar ones, to improve the effectiveness of their arts. I suspect that some teachers, especially in the less recent past, also made efforts to pass on to selected students teachings that had nothing directly to do with martial arts but that had everything to do with developing an understanding of oneself.

The two parts of martial arts training that may be the most closely related to the earlier Taoist teachings are concerned with the focusing of energy and the attitude to one's opponent.

Clearly it is advantageous to any fighter to be able to focus the maximum amount of energy at a particular point in the body. Secondly, if you can cultivate an attitude of separateness from the threatening advance or appearance of an opponent, this too is an advantage. Any method that could effectively influence energy flow in the body could contribute to achieving both of these aims.

The founder of Pakua, Tung Hai Ch'uan, learned about and was influenced by Taoism, the *I Ching*, the Five Elements, and martial arts training. Implicit in his teachings was the alchemical idea of the transformation of energy. But on their own such ideas are flat, two-dimensional: they need a living teacher to change them into the realities of experience. There do not seem to be many such teachers around. What there is today is a host of books. Can there ever have been a time when there were so many books about how to achieve a control of internal energy? I doubt it. It is not just a matter of improved printing technology and quicker means of distribution: there is a real demand for such books.

This is in stark contrast to the days of the early Taoists and their immediate descendants. In those times, such teachings were hidden. This may confront us with a further question. Were such things hidden because of cultural customs or political objectives? Or was there another reason, such as the idea of a limited amount of 'gold' to go around? If you have a large bank-vault of gold and share it out with one million people, each person will receive very little. What could he or she do with it? Our society is very strongly influenced by ideas of 'equality'. Equality of earning power, equality of the sexes and races, equality of opportunity, and other equalities are all extolled and pursued. So can there be an equality of wisdom, an equality of understanding?

When a snake is ready, it sheds its skin. If you see the old skin, you know that a snake was there. The real snake has gone but there is the skin, proving that a snake was there; you know that if you search long enough you may find a snake. Perhaps all these books are like the snake's skin. Many people say that they are looking for snakes. They find the skin. Then they find another skin, and another. Soon many give up, losing heart and interest. But perhaps the people who continue to search may eventually find a real, living snake. Was there equality of opportunity here? More or less. But what was not 'equal' was the being, the make-up, of the people who began searching for the snake. Once again we find echoes of such an idea in the Christian parable of the sower. The fertile ground, as opposed to the poor ground and the weed-infested ground, represents the being of the person who hears the Word, receives the seed.

It appears that once an idea has been released into society by a teacher – for instance, the concept of the Yin and the Yang – it inevitably becomes distorted. The teacher achieves a moment of deep understanding, and in attempting to pass this on, however approximately, to a student, he uses a concept, a parable, a movement sequence, a symbol. This is never the experience itself, but a representation of it. Suppose that he understands that there is a limited amount of understanding 'gold' to go round. This idea may be understood by his closest disciples, but it also leaks out to the ones who do not understand it in themselves, but only in their minds, their intellects. They in turn repeat it to their pupils, and somehow it turns into the idea that the teachings are secret. It began as the idea that only a limited number can understand, and it is changed into the idea that secrecy is very important. The way has been forgotten; simply dogma remains.

Continuing on this theme, we may note also that secrecy is (or was) a big feature of martial arts tradition. Martial arts techniques were kept in the family or in the clan. This tradition may have begun for very ordinary, practical reasons. For instance, if your enemy knows your methods he can be better prepared to face you in combat – so you do not reveal your methods to anyone who is outside the family, not even to your in-laws! Suppose this traditional practice comes into contact with the debased idea of a limited amount of 'gold' that has turned into the idea of the importance of secrecy. The two ideas reinforce one another. You have a philosophical justification for your strategic attitude. Old and recent history contain many examples of religious and philosophical and scientific ideas being used for personal and national ends – often with dire consequences for all concerned. In this way, a teaching that originated as an effort to elevate humankind is changed into a means of bringing humankind down. Small wonder, then, that the early Taoists kept their lifestyle and training secret! They had more than one good reason for so doing.

In some of the accounts of the lifestyle that have been published or openly taught, there is one key concept. This is the
concept of hierarchy. 'Hierarchy' is not now a politically correct
word: it militates against the current vogue word 'equality'. The
British royal family have been reported, photographed, spied
on, and generally brought into disrepute in a way that would
have been unthinkable a few decades ago. Teachers, parents,
the police, the government, all people in authority are afforded
little respect. Whether they deserve respect is another question.
But the very notion of someone or something more important
than the famous 'man in the street', of someone in some sense
'better' than someone else, is anathema these days. There are
many examples of this anathema's being contradicted, even so.
The media is full of cases where it is a 'shame' or scandal that
someone has been treated in this or that fashion, and this
implies some kind of standard, which in turn implies a sense of
hierarchy.

The Taoist philosophy contained this concept. The Taoists, or
the Chinese physicians, or the antecedents of both of these
groups, discovered that within the human frame there are different energies: *chi* expressed vital energy; *ching* vitality; and
shen spirit. Although not expressed in numerical terms, *shen* or
spirit was seen as the acme of human energy, the highest
energy. In terms of the spectrum we could say it was in the
ultra-violet range and beyond. Lower down came *ching* and *chi*.
The Taoists taught that *shen* in some sense 'ruled' or 'governed'
the other energies, and each lower energy ruled the one below
it. So a hierarchy existed. If one element, one energy of the hierarchy, was weak or malfunctioning, the whole was affected. But
the most important to the general 'health' was the *shen* or spirit.

This concept also found its application in the political field.
The Taoists taught that if the Emperor was inattentive and
uncaring, then his ministers would neglect their duties, and in
turn their underlings would be careless, and this would affect
the merchants, and in turn the peasants, and soon the whole
country would fall into ruin. So as it is in the single human
being, so it is in the country at large. A hierarchy exists between
humans and heaven. Disturb it at your peril.

The Taoist philosophy had as one of its aims the unhindered
and direct exchange of energies between the different levels.
The relationship between *chi* and the lower-energy-substance

Blood is an example. The Chinese notion of Blood was not only blood itself but the functions of blood. *Chi* helped to govern the Blood, and the Blood – if well regulated – could help to nourish the *chi*. Taoist training tried to facilitate this. Suppose, then, that through the Taoist lifestyle and training this hierarchy in the human frame could be brought to optimum condition. What for?

This is an important question, and one that is worth thinking about. In my own experience, coming into contact with hundreds of martial artists, would-be martial artists, searchers after secrets, and so on, the question does come up. People would telephone me, or call at my shop, or come to my classes, looking for something. Many of them leaned towards martial arts with Taoist connections, such as Tai Chi Chuan. You could say that they were looking for a live snake and had found a few snake skins. They wanted to know if I knew where the live snake was. I did what I could at the time. It is a dilemma. It is a dilemma because people in general do not understand that you cannot change and stay the same as you are. If you asked one hundred people to get up half an hour earlier every morning for three months, without fail, almost none of them could. They would not be able to change, even to that extent. If you pointed this out to them after the ninety days, they would all find a good reason or excuse or justification for not managing it. What few would realize is that the important thing is that they should know they cannot. So if they cannot get up half an hour earlier in the morning, what is the point of dreaming about Taoist transformation? Taoist philosophy needs more discipline than getting up at 7am instead of 7.30am. But people always want something big and challenging to do: they do not want to be 'faithful in small things'.

So one of the facts all this shows is that many people, in approaching Taoism or Pakua or Tai Chi, are looking for a miracle. They do not want the hard work. The live snake they are seeking is a miracle. So our next thought should be: am I justified in looking for a miracle? Are you? In my view, you are justified. You are alchemically justified. The Taoist theme of alchemy was concerned with the miracle of turning 'lead' into 'gold', of turning the ordinary level of experience into the gold of understanding. If you have seen the film *Treasure of the Sierra Madre* you may recall that when the small gang, led by

Humphrey Bogart, accumulated their gold dust, but then they were stopped and attacked by a band of ruffians and their gold dust thrown to the winds. Their attackers did not know what gold dust was. We find ourselves in a similar position. The first miracle we need is to recognize gold when we find it. 'Gold is where you find it' is not an idle statement. So this is our first hurdle: the recognition of gold.

Pakua presents us with many ideas, movements, techniques, and suggestions. If what I have written is only approximately correct, then there is 'gold in them thar hills' of Pakua. My suggestion is that you see Pakua and train at Pakua as a means of understanding. Study it for what it can teach you about yourself. Do not see it as an end in itself: if you do that, you turn your back on the purpose for which it was created.

The ideas of the Taoists and the Yin-Yang school spread into different areas of Chinese life. One notable example is the field of painting. Whereas the martial artists applied these ideas to movement and space, the painters applied them to objects and space. The name of the principle used here is *k'ai-ho* or 'expanding and collecting'. This idea has been used by some Tai Chi and Pakua students and given the name in English of Opening and Closing. It is clearly an example of Yin and Yang at work.

In acclaimed Chinese works of art there is always a balance between space and objects. Artists speak of the tension between the two, or the way the one affects the other. Whether the space is sky or simply a wash of colour as a background, and whether the objects are mountains, animals or shoots of bamboo, the balance is always there. The detailed impressions experienced by people who are interested in art are beyond those of us who are not, but it is not difficult to appreciate that there is a tangible contact between space and objects. This is carried further by the idea that where there is opening or expanding there is almost a need for contracting, closing or collecting. Put simply, space calls for an object and an object calls for space.

An artist experiences these 'calls' simultaneously – that is, in giving space he feels the need for an object, and vice versa. In performing an expanding movement in Pakua, the student is aware of the coming contraction. In reaching out with Dragon Turns Its Head, he or she is mindful of the oncoming crossing and folding of the arms. Such an awareness, both on the part of the artists and the Pakua student, indicates a step up the ladder of perception. A beginner in either field is less likely to be aware of this. In making one movement, a beginner is usually very much preoccupied with that movement. What comes next usually presents itself as another quite separate step. This is all part of being a beginner, of course, but it is what causes the hesitation, the awkwardness in the movements. The student does not see a Form as a flowing whole which expresses the principle of *k'ai-ho*.

In paintings there is also the principle, found in Pakua and martial arts in general, that there should be a balance between movement and stillness. For example, in the picture by Ch'i Pai-Shih called *Cow and Willows*, the cow is depicted at the bottom as a rotund solid with long thin strands of foliage rising beside it. Two tiny birds pass overhead. The rest is space. The solid quality of the cow gives an impression of stillness, and the foliage and birds an impression of movement. In martial arts the stillness is found in the focus of attention and the maintaining of the centre of gravity around which the movements are made. In Tai Chi, for example, what gives the slow arm movements their special quality is the firm, rooted centre, going down from the abdomen to the feet. If you try to make such movements with what we might call 'weak legs', the arms immediately lose something. Strengthen the legs and the arms change at once.

In painting we have a finished object. In the martial arts we have movement. Yet the same principles apply. As a topical footnote I should add that a movement therapist whom I respect told me that she has numbers of Tai Chi students coming to her for treatment. These people have taken the principle of rooting, going down, but have forgotten about going up. They are virtually collapsing, and appear at her door with urgent calls for realignment. This falls within the area of *k'ai-ho*. With ascent there is descent. With descent there is ascent. Nowhere in Tai Chi does it say *only go down*. The head should be suspended 'as if by a single hair', implying a movement upwards. Simultaneous up-and-down in the body means an optimum balance. This applies to Pakua. At the same time simultaneous opposite movement is not restricted to the vertical, but could appear too in lateral movement. Move or turn right should mean pay some attention too to the left. Nothing is completely Yin or Yang; there is, or should be, always an element of the other in the principal direction. This Yin-Yang balance is found naturally in the world of nature. As civilized people we have fallen into a narrow, limited level of being, which not only does not recognize the existence of three forces (see page 125), but needs reminding of the existence of even two. To *only go down* means to be aware of the existence of only one. In an objective sense this places us on a level of being below that of a normal human being.

As for the present Western state of the martial arts, and Pakua in particular, there are comparatively large numbers of people who have a high level of physical skill. Some of these have devoted long periods in their lives to training and refining. When you see them in action, you realize that in their bodies they have grasped a great deal concerning the principles I have described. A smaller number among them have also studied intellectually the theories, the history and the ramifications of their chosen art. What has rarely taken place, however, is that the combination of these two aspects – physical and intellectual – has brought about a certain something hard to put into one word. The word *wisdom* or the word *understanding* could be used, but what do they mean? It is something which, as a teenager, I myself hoped to find in martial arts. This is acceptable as an expectation because the message is there, in martial arts. Unfortunately, I did not find the messenger, and had to look outside the martial arts world to do so. That said, the martial arts do modify character to some extent, sometimes for the better but not always. Sometimes the success and special abilities that the martial arts can bring simply give people a bigger ego than they originally had.

Although it is true that Western people, including myself, do not understand Eastern people, it does not mean that we are unable to judge the martial arts of the East, or Eastern instructors. We judge them not on the basis of Eastern culture and background but from our own perspective. This is the only one we have. These arts have come and taken root in the West. If they have grown, it has been on Western soil, with Western nourishment, and their taste has been experienced by Western palates.

Chapter 10

Pakua and the *I Ching*

Today many people know something of the *I Ching* or Book of Changes. It derives from an ancient method of divination that was eventually systematized. The basic diagrams of the system are called trigrams, of which there are eight. Each trigram consists of different arrangements of unbroken and broken lines, as in figure 90. Later the trigrams were combined in hexagrams; that is, diagrams with six lines, as in figure 91. There are 64 of these in all. The *I Ching* was revered by Confucius and has been used for divination for centuries. There are established and accepted interpretations and there are independent interpretations drawn by individual persons who consult it. Its popularity in the West was first enhanced by the interest shown in it by the famous analytical psychologist Jung. The names of the eight basic trigrams are:

QIAN   GEN   LI   KAN   XUN   ZHEN   KUN   DUI

The long unbroken line is seen as a Yang, strong line, and the broken line as a Yin, weak line. The interpretation of the arrangements of the lines into varieties of three demands considerable study. For one thing, it is necessary to learn the Chinese attitude to the lines and their meanings of Yin and Yang, weak and strong. A simplistic and unthinking approach is useless. In studying the *I Ching* it is essential to get behind first thoughts and go deeper and deeper into the subtleties. If a strong line is the bottom line, one conclusion is drawn; if a strong line is the top line, another conclusion is reached; if all three lines are strong, this is a fully Yang or masculine or strong position; if they are all weak, a completely different position is indicated.

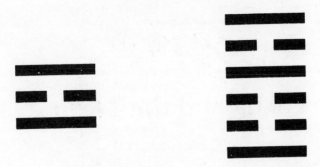

Figure 90 The Li trigram – one of the   Figure 91 Trigrams combined to give
Pa Kua   a hexagram

But, in any case, the first significance you afford to the words *strong* and *weak* may not necessarily be the most appropriate.

In keeping with Chinese tradition, the venerable nature of the *I Ching* and its trigrams and hexagrams resulted in its being applied to all important matters in human affairs. In medicine and what we might loosely call physical culture, the organs of the body, the energies of the body, the parts of the body, and so forth, were all thus linked with the trigrams in a certain order. In the Western way of thinking we might not see how some of these connections can be justified. But whether we see it or not, in Pakua we have an internal martial art that is based entirely on the trigrams of the *I Ching*. In other words, Pakua did not start off as one thing and then have parts of the *I Ching* tacked on to it for reasons of prestige (a practice not unheard of in Chinese cultural history). So for the moment it is better to suspend judgement, study the subject, and wait and see.

Like another venerable tool in Chinese philosophy, the Five Elements, the trigrams are often arranged in a circle to show their cyclic relationship in any one setting. We have seen that Pakua students walk the circle. In the more theoretical study of the art, the trigrams are arranged around the circle as shown in figure 92. Opinions about how this should be done may vary, but the fundamental cyclic idea is the same in many martial arts.

LI	Hawk
ZHEN	Dragon
KAN	Snake

Figure 92 Eight trigrams – Pa Kua – arranged in a circle

DUI	Monkey
XUN	Phoenix
GEN	Bear
QIAN	Lion
KUN	Unicorn

In this arrangement the trigrams are related to the Pakua animals whose characteristics are echoed as it were by the trigram concerned. For instance, Qian, which consists of three solid Yang lines, is related to the lion, the king of beasts in our Western view, and full of powerful Yang qualities. At the opposite pole we find Kun, the unicorn, with three broken lines representing the shy, mythical creature with soft, feminine qualities.

The movements of Pakua are in turn related to the animals. The lion Palms or hand techniques are the most powerful, and the unicorn Palms the most soft and fluid. So we have a continuous picture of relationships in which the fundamental trigrams are connected to the eight animals and the animals determine the eight fundamental Palm Changes of Pakua. In walking the circle, the Pakua student passes through the eight trigrams and performs the techniques appropriate to each trigram. This should not be interpreted too literally. In other words, in walking the circle the student does not, in one cycle, perform eight techniques. Rather he or she will walk the circle several times, focusing on one change, for instance Kan, the snake, and rehearsing those movements. This is evidence of a simple deviation of the theory from the practice. It contrasts with the cycles of energy movement through the body, with cycles related to the seasons and times of day, and with all (as it were) 'fixed' cycles.

The eight Palm Changes echo the basic idea of *change* in the *I Ching*. In interpreting the *I Ching* and in following the fluctuations of Yin and Yang, this is an important element. The art of Pakua has fluid and ingenious ways of moving from one Palm Change to another. These echo the subtlety of the *I Ching* interpretation, in which a trigram has its own meaning but is also shaded or coloured by the trigrams on both sides of it. A student carries out the Palm Change associated, for example, with the dragon, which we can designate the core Change, but as he begins it he has just left another Palm Change, and as he ends it he begins yet another Palm Change. Returning to the *I Ching*, we find that the influence of the preceding and following trigrams or hexagrams colour the interpretation of the one that is the main subject of consideration. What comes before and what comes after leavens the core. Likewise, the middle of the hexagram is coloured by the bottom and top lines.

In performing the movements of any animal or Palm Change, the trigrams can thus help in the interpretation of the movement. Because six of the Palm Changes include elements that consist of a mingling of Yin and Yang, in soft and hard, in coiling or linear action, the body should adapt to these indications. This must happen willy-nilly because it is governed by the muscular and joint fitness of the student, as well as by the actions that are called for. If a student knows that he or she must do a Yin-type action but also knows that the next movement is a Yang action, the knowledge will inevitably colour his or her activity. It is part of the skill and understanding of oneself that Pakua requires to be able to do the changes, the crossovers, from one movement to another from one Palm Change to another, with dexterity. It is a considerable challenge.

Before moving on to another aspect of the trigrams, let us examine a Palm Change in some detail keeping the above considerations in mind.

Take the movement called Black Dragon Turns Its Head Right. You are walking the circle clockwise, as in figure 93. The posture of the body is relatively open, Yang, on the right side, and relatively closed on the left side, Yin. You approach the

Palm Change, knowing that it is coming. You are going to do a much more Yin movement, closing the feet into a V step, crossing the arms close to the body, in several stages which in reality consist of one smooth movement. The fact that you are going to do this change influences you, even if you do not consciously experience it. So as you bring the left foot round into a V step, figure 94, try to be aware of the activity of your muscles, their state of tension, and your thoughts, if any. Do you 'know' what you are going to do? You step out away from the centre, as in figure 95, opening a little more, Yang, and then make another V step, Yin, crossing the arms close to the body, Yin, and coiling in towards your own centre, Yin, like a spring ready to be released. If you do this movement slowly and carefully you will experience the way the body prepares itself for the next movement and gives up the previous movement. So now the Yin

Figure 93 Black Dragon posture

Figure 94 V step

Figure 95 T step

Figure 96 Opening out

'spring' is about to release itself into the Yang turn. Your arms open, Yang, towards the left, as in figure 96, and then you step out into the first posture, this time walking anticlockwise, more Yang than in the previous movement, and open on the left side, more closed on the right.

Note that the movements of the Palm Change each had their own Yin-Yang validity, and the whole Change moved the Yang emphasis from the right to the left side of the body – that is, reversed the Yin-Yang emphasis. Within the whole Change were many, many adjustments involving the whole body: the muscles, the breathing, the 'intention'. These may seem to you like minutiae at present, but if you try to take an interest in them you will find it a rewarding endeavour. Since the movement itself was a dragon movement, it should contain all the power and lithe quality that we associate with the creature.

Of course the speed of body movement is greater than the speed of our normal thought processes. The theoretical considerations of changes from one trigram to another seem long and laborious in comparison with physical movement. But with patience you can break down each second of your movement and experience it in quite a different way. Eventually such analyses have to make way for smooth performance, but with study and training this performance can exemplify the sum total of the analyses.

In their reflections and cogitations, the more scholarly Pakua practitioners extended the use of the trigrams to include different parts of the body. One interpretation is shown below:

QIAN	head
LI	heart
KUN	abdomen (middle)
XUN	lower vertebrae
GEN	neck
ZHEN	abdomen (left side)
DUI	abdomen (right side)
KAN	kidneys

This arrangement is interpreted variously but as in Traditional Chinese Medicine it can be thought of as revealing a distribution of energy.

This same medical theory divides the influences in a human being's life into two main phases: before the human is born

(Pre-birth) and after the human is born (Post-birth). From one point of view, the Pre-birth phase is pure: it does not come into direct contact with any of the 'corrupting' and contradictory influences of life in the outside world. The eight trigrams showing the Pre-birth position are as in figure 97.

The eight-trigram arrangement for the Post-birth condition is shown in figure 98. The theory additionally points out that although there are corrupting influences of life in the outside world, there may also be weaknesses and defects of one kind or another in the Pre-birth condition.

Through Pakua, some practitioners believe that a bridge between the two conditions can be made – so that Post-birth work can remedy defects in the Pre-birth condition, the needful characteristics of the Pre-birth condition can be introduced into the Post-birth condition, and that in this way the two may be integrated. Pre-birth is described as Yin, and Post-birth as Yang. When the two arrangements are placed one inside the other, the result appears as in figure 99.

It may not be too fanciful to see that one aspect of this type of arrangement calls to mind the Biblical saying: 'The wolf also shall dwell with the lamb, and the leopard shall lie down with the kid' (Isaiah 11:6). Fanciful or not, the arrangement does

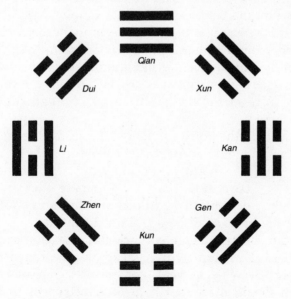

Figure 97 Pre-birth Pa Kua arrangement

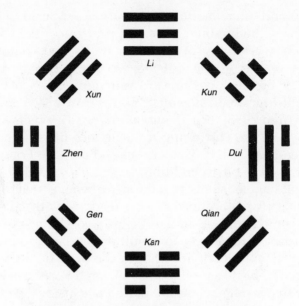

Figure 98 Post-birth Pa Kua arrangement

suggest the bringing together of qualities, in one and the same person, that may at first sight seem to be mutually exclusive. For instance, how can the wolf quality in a person live in close proximity with the lamb quality? On a simple physical level we can say that a person has to be able to evince great strength, self-confidence and power, like a wolf, together with playfulness, softness and innocence, like a lamb; to display the lithe, sinuous, flickering movements of the snake, as well as the lumbering force of the bear; and so on, through combination after combination.

On the level of the body's functioning, the arrangements suggest that the different parts of the body, which may be naturally weaker or stronger in any given individual, should be evened out – that one part should not predominate over another, be exceptionally weak or strong in comparison with another; that qualities present at birth or acquired during one's life can be balanced out. The challenge is there. Pakua says it can be met. In the simplest of terms this is readily comprehensible. If a person is born with a weak constitution, the mere fact of training in Pakua may well help to remedy this. In such an instance the Pre-birth condition has been ameliorated by the

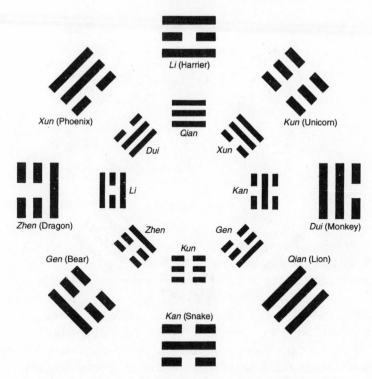

Figure 99 Pre- and Post-birth arrangements combined

Post-birth. Conversely, for example, Sun Lu Tang was born into appalling Post-birth conditions but his inborn capacity to face hardship, to work and study, overcame these conditions.

In taking this position, Pakua presents itself as a Way, in the sense of trying to understand what I am and what my relationship is with the universe. The compass, as it were, on this journey, is the Pakua of the *I Ching*.

PRACTICAL

But this is not a book about philosophy, and because there are many books about the philosophy and meaning of the *I Ching*, let us return instead to a simple and perhaps simplistic use of the trigrams in relation to movement.

Take the second Palm Change, which begins just like the first Palm Change, and analyse each movement. From this analysis

Figure 100 V step

we will select an appropriate trigram. We begin by walking the circle anticlockwise; the left hand points towards the centre of the circle, and the right hand 'guards' the elbow and ribcage.

The first new movement is to turn in with the right foot into a V step, as in figure 100. In this instance the turned-in feet indicate a closed, Yin line: two broken lines at the bottom. The middle, with closed-in groin and abdomen, indicate a Yin: two broken lines in the middle. The top, more open to the left, indicates a Yang: one line. But this is where the analysis becomes interesting. Although Yin can be interpreted as 'weak', here it clearly does not mean 'weak' in the accepted sense because the V step is a coiled-up strong leg position, possessing big potential. Likewise the groin and mid-section are full of potential power. The arms also express, to some extent, the potential of the foot and leg movements, so that Yang here is clear. We begin to see, then, that the meaning of Yin is wider and deeper than it superficially appears. It brings to mind the saying that when a Yin or Yang process reaches its extreme, the next phase of the pattern is the beginning of its opposite: extreme Yin is potential Yang, and extreme Yang is potential Yin.

For the second movement, continuing Black Dragon Turns Its Head to the Left, the left foot steps out away from the centre of the circle, opening up the feet, Yang, and the mid-section, Yang, and the arms even more, Yang.

The third movement, beginning Hawk Flies Up into the Sky, once again has a V step, Yin, closed-in abdomen, Yin, and crossed arms close to the body, Yin. This indicates being even more potentially 'wound up' than previously. A completely closed Yin position waiting to be let go. Bearing in mind the notion that the previous trigram (in this case in the form of a movement) colours and to some extent prepares for the next one, we see strong Yang leading to strong Yin.

The fourth movement, continuing the Hawk change, brings the feet alongside one another, close, and therefore Yin. But here the more careful analysis brings us up against another consideration. The previous movement with the V step was with the feet closed at the front, Yin, but the heels splayed wide at the back, Yang. The abdomen and chest were closed at the front, Yin, but open at the back, Yang. Similarly the shoulders, closed front and open back. So we cannot escape the thought that *any* strong Yang or Yin position produces its opposite position somewhere in the body.

You may well ask in this case if our analysis holds water. It does, if you relate your Yin-Yang analysis to the *intention*. This means that although a position of the body may display both Yin and Yang features, if these are considered in relationship to the question, 'What am I trying to do?', then the relative importances of the counterbalancing Yin and Yang are clear. In the case of the position with the V step, the intention was to coil up ready for release in the next movement, so the Yin of the V step is more important than the Yang of the V step. This is a simplistic demonstration of the principle that Yin and Yang constitute the *tao*, if *tao* is interpreted to mean 'direction' – in this case 'intention'.

Returning to the fourth movement, one hand is fired upwards and the other is thrust downwards, opening and closing together. But as the main movement of the body is down into a crouch, we can conclude Yin at the top. The mid-section is open, Yang.

The fifth movement begins the White Snake change. The legs spread wide, the feet are turned out, Yang. The arms are akimbo, Yang, and the chest open, Yang. But the overall posture is down, signifying Yin, so the generally Yang picture given by the open position of the body is balanced to some extent by this Yin consideration. We can see here how careful analysis of several factors, combined with an experienced 'feel' for what is going on, are what is needed.

The fifth movement speeds into Black Dragon Turns to the Right. Once again we have a Yin movement.

The sixth movement then shows a release of the Yin from the previous movement, and we turn right into a clockwise walk.

The above paragraphs may appear complicated at first, but they are not. You will soon see them clearly if you work through the thinking and analysis several times. To indicate how this analysis can be pursued in even more detail, let us take just the last two movements, as in figures 101 and 102. If you look at figure 103, and *do* it, not just think of it, you see that as you raise your arms across your body indicating Yang, from the previous very closed position indicating Yin, the right arm rises higher, more Yang, and the left arm is lower, more Yin. The chest raises itself a little, Yang, but the abdomen and legs hug the ground, Yin. As you move your arms over in an arc, to the right, this Yin-Yang situation changes with regard to the rising and falling of

Figure 101 More Yin position

Figure 102 More Yang position

Figure 103 Arms in intermediate Yin to Yang position

the arms and chest, so there is a rise from Yin to more Yang and a fall back to relative Yin again.

ADVICE

Do not be discouraged if it all seems rather complicated. All you need are a certain degree of visualization, some awareness of your body, and the ability to translate, however slowly, words into actions. When I was a youngster, books on Judo (for instance) were very sparely illustrated. To make use of a book meant that you had to visualize in order to try out what was written. I certainly did this hundreds of times, may be thousands.

Let us take an action – say, the one in the final paragraphs above. Your arms, crossed one over the other, rise from the left side of your ribcage, up above your head and down to the other side. This can be *visualized* as an arc. There is nothing difficult about it. Then as you do the movement, be aware of your ribcage and note that it does rise and fall with your arm movement. This is cultivating your basic awareness of movement. Remember that Yin is usually falling and Yang rising, and you have the picture:

Awareness – Visualization – Words

If you cultivate these capacities, you will see many ways in which the trigrams of the *I Ching* can be used to interpret your movements.

Chapter 11

Taoist Meditation

The Chinese author Chang Chung Yuan produced this translation from the writings of Chuang-tzu:

> If you put your body in the correct posture and concentrate on the One, the Heavenly Harmony will descend upon you. Hold on to your inner awareness and unify yourself with the Absolute. God will lodge within you, and you will abide with the Tao. This achievement will fill you with joy. You will be like the newly born calf, gazing but not seeking anything.

The light that shines forth from someone in this state is referred to by Chuang-tzu as 'the dragon'.

Such a passage is inspiring. It touches the reader and presents hope to the seeker of understanding. It is a typical pithy Chinese saying: almost every word is full of important background implications. It is like a worked diamond, a piece of fine craftsmanship, inspiring because it is so 'finished'. The viewer, the reader, can admire, can be inspired, even without knowing how the finished article was produced.

But there is some danger, as it were, in this experience. If someone believes that he or she understands the state described, is it true, or is it an illusion? It is one thing to be moved, but another to understand. To understand means to be able to enter into this state for oneself. To be moved means to partly share in the experience through one's own feelings. If you see an excellent performance of Pakua, you can be moved, you can admire. But you may not be able to perform Pakua in the same way.

Looking at the passage again, you should ask yourself how

you could 'put your body in the correct posture'. If you were to see a Taoist sage sitting or standing in 'the correct posture', and if you were to adopt what you hoped was the same posture, you could be sure that your posture would be merely an approximation. Teachers of the martial arts or any exercise system know how difficult pupils find it to reach even an approximation of the correct posture. One reason for this is that the correct posture is not just a question of coarse muscle use, it depends very much on how the performer feels *inside*. It is this correct feeling inside which takes time to discover. For instance, many people find it impossible to relax the lower back to any appreciable extent. Relaxation there can be achieved by a deeper perception of the state of the muscles of the torso, but it can be attained much more quickly and readily by having a different feeling, a feeling that is usually quite different from the ordinary feelings we experience daily. So perhaps the use of the word 'If' at the beginning of the passage is the most significant thing for us. 'If . . .'

Moving on to the next part of Chuang-tzu we read, '. . . and concentrate on the One'. 'If you . . . concentrate on the One.' If you can, that is what you will do; but if you cannot, how can you begin?

Nonetheless, if you carry out the first requirements, 'the Heavenly Harmony will descend upon you'. Leaving aside the question of whether and how it might happen for the moment, this final part of the first sentence shows the Yin-Yang principle at work. The meditator has to prepare himself or herself, quite actively, with correct posture and 'concentration', which indicates a strong Yang effort. But for the 'Heavenly harmony' to come down, he or she must become Yin in relation to the energy descending, Yang. Be prepared, but as a human, Yin, in relation to Heaven, Yang.

'Hold on to your inner awareness . . .' First you must actually have inner awareness. What does this mean? What is awareness? It must be akin to the senses, such as seeing or touching. But one thing it is not. It is not *thinking*. In all methods of meditation the problem of inner chatter, intrusive imagination, daydreaming comes up. There are various means of coping with it. When the mind is quiet, awareness can become more available. In Tai Chi the awareness is focused on the correct, slow movement, and later, perhaps, the breathing and relaxation.

'And unify yourself with the Absolute.' Through holding on to your awareness, this unification with the Absolute is said to be possible. What this means cannot be described in words.

'God will lodge within you, and you will abide with the Tao.' What this means is also indescribable – but we may suppose that you will abide with the Tao because God is there. Only if God is there can you abide with the Tao.

The remainder of the passage describes how you will feel, and what the results of this experience will be. The Yang experience will result in the Yin experiences. The latter can be compared with something more or less recognizable by most people – joy, innocence, and lack of desire. The deeper experience which produced it cannot be spoken about.

An important fact has been illustrated. We can say that in all true Ways there are three divisions: theoretical, philosophical and practical. For us the passage from Chuang-tzu is theoretical. It is not philosophical in the sense that it portrays a logical, arguable structure; nor is it practical in the sense that we can instantly go out and do it. But it *is* practical in the sense that it presents a series of steps, causes and effects, albeit so very broadly drawn that, as we have seen, they do not convey anything one can 'do', so they are much more genuinely theoretical. Even when such steps are broken down into more detailed description, they remain theoretical, bordering on the philosophical.

For instance, one approach is connected with the idea of alchemy that I referred to earlier. Instead of the word *gold* the expression 'inner elixir' is used. This inner elixir of understanding is, in theory, produced by the action of three energies: *chi*, *ching* and *shen*. *Chi* is related to the energy of the breath, *ching* to the vitality of sexual energy, and *shen* to consciousness. By influencing these energies, the inner elixir can be produced. When we read fragments of Taoist lore relating to breathing exercises, it is to this purpose that the exercises are applied. References to sexual energy transformations are similarly concerned with the inner elixir. One effect of such practices is to reveal the consciousness that existed before a person was born – a consciousness that has indeed been covered over by the fact of being born and of existing in the world. This possibility is one also put forward by Pakua practitioners, notably by Sun Lu Tang.

Another fragment of Taoist teaching says that a human is a microcosm existing in a macrocosm, the universe. To find the inner elixir is to begin to be related to the macrocosm. Because the universe consists of the Five Elements – wood, fire, earth, metal and water – and because the inner organs of kidney, liver, lung, spleen and heart each correspond to one of the elements, and because again each element is 'produced' by the one preceding it, the energy motion is circular. This idea is closely connected to the Pakua practice of walking the circle.

These explanations are all very interesting. At the same time they are tantalizing. One is tempted to say, 'Yes, but how do you *do* it? So far it is all theoretical.' The difficulty does not lie in the material, the explanations, but in ourselves. There is a story about a promising pupil who was accepted by a Taoist master to study meditation with him. One day the pupil felt an enormous pulse of energy inside him, as if struck by lightning. All his normal perceptions disappeared for about half an hour or more. When he came to himself he felt purified, a new man. He spoke to the master about his experience and the master replied that he had had that experience hundreds of times and had learned to ignore it! No doubt it took the pupil some time to reach the same attitude . . . The story shows us something about the differences between people. One man has an amazing experience and understands where it belongs in himself. Another has a similar experience and is bowled over by it. This means that the two people are *not the same*. This is something we are not accustomed to think about. It is not part of our intellectual or emotional make-up. We tend to think of people as more or less the same. In particular, someone who takes an interest in the contents of this book might well think of himself or herself as more or less on a par with the people described in it – or if not quite on a par, then with a bit of effort he or she could be so. A few more words of explanation will surely bring full understanding.

That is not the case. It is something we referred to earlier. We need to begin to know how we are, and what we are, before we can understand what we might become. That is the hardest obstacle for us. What we read in Taoist literature refers to people who are different from us – not just a little different, but very different. The literature is written by people who are different, and what they write is mainly directed at people who are sufficiently prepared to be able to understand it – that is, not at ordinary people. People familiar with the New Testament will remember that Jesus spoke in parables to the ordinary people because they were not, in martial arts parlance, inner-chamber disciples and would not understand what he said to his disciples.

The Role of Forms

You may well be wondering if I am doing my best to discourage you. That is certainly not the case. If you are willing to accept that we need first to know how we are now and what we are now, then a start can be made. Taoists contributed to the formation of martial arts styles, and Pakua, as we have seen, is one of these styles. If you begin to study one of the Forms, such as the eight Palm Changes of this book, you will immediately begin to discover how you are now, and what you are.

You will discover how difficult you find it to remember the movements. Time and again you will find your feet, arms, head and trunk in the wrong place, at the wrong inclination, with the wrong degree of tension. And sometimes you will find that they are right. If you continue to train and study, and find that you still keep doing things wrong, it is time to pause and reflect. Why? Your reflections are your own.

If your reflections are honest, you will admit that you do not know how to produce the desired actions, in the desired way. And you will be forced to admit that *this is how you are*. The result of this admission can be a new appreciation, a new evaluation. And it is this new evaluation, this new thought and feeling, which can help you to do things better.

Just now I have a pupil who has tried to learn Chen-style Tai Chi from me for about two years. He has battled on and was near the end of learning the combined Form. Today he came for a lesson and finally realized that he hadn't the faintest idea of how to move suitably for the Chen style. But he was willing to go back to the beginning, to listen to what I was saying, and try it. If he remembers that he hasn't the faintest idea, he will improve; if he forgets, he will go back to the way he was doing things before. His admission produced a different evaluation, which means a new feeling. This new feeling is one of the keys.

It is very difficult to recognize the value of a new feeling without the assistance of a teacher. That is part of the alchemy of study. Many people have experienced the feeling of tranquillity which comes from Tai Chi Chuan. And they have also experienced the disappearance of this feeling.

So Forms can not only produce a change in how we feel but also correspond to a manual of instruction. If we were men and women of Tao we would be able to do the Forms, perhaps not need them. But because we are not, the Forms – which are externally applied like poultices or medicines – can produce changes. Willingness to learn, inside, combined with the Forms, outside, act together. Slowly, the Form learned as a beginner, Form number 1, produces another Form, learned as a more experienced beginner, Form number 2. If Form number 2 is not forgotten, it can lead to Form number 3, and so on. It is all the 'same' Form but the performer changes – which means the Form changes. Each 'new' Form, like the new skin of the snake, is not just physical movement: it depends on new thoughts and feelings, as well as the action of nerves and muscles and joints. So the role of Forms can be like a catalyst, something which in its ideal existence does not change, but helps to produce change. In a broad sense it is part of Taoist meditation in movement. To persist in such an approach will result, inevitably, in glimpses of the truth and the meaning of some of the Taoist literature. You will understand some of what is meant because you will have experienced it for yourself.

A simple example of the process of learning can help to clarify this. If you begin to learn the first Palm Change, either from a book or teacher, you first have to remember. This is usually a slow, mental process. If you are someone who can watch and quickly copy a movement, this initial mental process is left out. But in both cases there will be points about the movement that you will forget, or, in the instance of a quick copier, which you will miss. In any event you will have to return, more than once, to the example presented to you, and even have it explained to you and corrected. Then, still, after all this, you will make mistakes. But the point at issue here is in the nature of the mistakes. What happens is that the mistakes become smaller, fewer, and less significant. As time passes and training time accumulates, you will have to think and observe less. Your performance will become more automatic. This can be designated Form 1. To a complete newcomer you will look like someone who 'knows' the first Palm Change – although to yourself you will admit that whereas you know it on one level, you do not know it on a deeper level. You look at the more advanced people, at the teacher, and what you see confirms your view.

At this stage you realize that what Master Un Ho Bun called the 'small points' are missing. (Master Un is a Kung Fu teacher who talked with me, taught me and advised me during the 1970s; he wrote books on Praying Mantis and Pak Mei styles.) Your Form is technically correct but too bland. For instance, it may lack the small 'winding up' movements that should occur at the end of each turning or twisting movement of the Palm Changes. If you continue to train and study, incorporating the small points in your Form, what emerges can be designated Form 2.

What happens between Form 1 and Form 2 is that your focus changes. The big points are no longer of primary concern; the small points are primary. Then you may begin to question the amount of energy you expend in doing the Form. In all probability you will find that you use too much. This calls into question your attitude. The study becomes more psychological. You need to talk to senior students and of course to a teacher to obtain their advice. You need to ask yourself why you are doing the Form; what is the purpose. If you succeed in resolving this question and reduce your energy output, what may then emerge can be designated Form 3.

It is impossible to say how many such new Forms may be needed. My first Tai Chi teacher told me of a monk in Taiwan who performed only two movements. He claimed that from these two movements he received as much as someone who taught the whole of the Yang-style Long Form. Such a state of affairs comes from being able to look inside, be aware, and find what is really taking place in the field of energy, impressions and attention. It is so intimate that it is probably true to say that only with a teacher can the majority of students find it.

Chapter 12

Beyond Theory

Higher Understanding

The movement of the *chi* from the lower *tantien* to the middle *tantien* and back, in a continuous cycle, is also best studied with a teacher. It is called the Lesser (or Smaller or Microcosmic) Circulation. A teacher is essential because of the subtlety of the action, and because of the possible danger in releasing energy that is completely unfamiliar to a student. No exercises or activities of this nature exist in a vacuum, and a student can find himself or herself in a situation like the sorcerer's apprentice who was able to set off a magic process but could not stop it. Several writers on the subject of Chi Kung, and a number of people I have met, have reported some bad experiences that came to students who dabbled in Chi Kung on their own.

The Lesser Circulation is prominent in martial arts and Taoist teaching, but is by no means confined to China. In the book *The Persian Sufis* by Cyprian Rice (George Allen & Unwin, London, 1965), the author quotes from a 13th-century Sufi classic, *Najmeddin Daya*:

> Laying his hands on his thighs, let him stir up his heart to wakefulness, keeping a guard on his eyes. Then with profound veneration he should say aloud, '*La Ilaha Illa'llah*'. The *La Ilaha* should be fetched from the root of the navel, and the *Illa'llah* drawn into the heart, so that the powerful effects of the *Zikr* [*dhikr*] may make themselves felt in all the limbs and organs.

The 'root of the navel' and the 'heart' referred to here are close enough to the lower and middle *tantiens* to be taken as the same. The passage goes on to speak of the feelings of the Sufi as he goes through his *Zikr*. He is advised to lose his sense of attachment and to focus on the love of God. This introduces an element not featured in Taoist texts on meditation that I have seen myself: feeling, in the way that it is spoken about in Christian and Islamic texts. That is not to say that such ideas do not exist. It may be that they are taken for granted, or rather that it is assumed that before even undertaking the Lesser Circulation, a student has already gone through a period of preparation.

In the Christian mystic tradition, the book *Writings from the Philokalia on the Prayer of The Heart*, translated by E Kadloubovsky and GEH Palmer (Faber & Faber, London, 1951), quotes:

> Collect your mind, lead it into the path of the breath, along which the air enters in, constrain it to enter the heart together with the inhaled air, and keep it there. Keep it there, but do not leave it silent and idle; instead give it the following prayer: 'Lord Jesus Christ, Son of God, have mercy upon me.'

Clearly it is not the 'air' that is led into the 'heart' but what the Chinese would call the 'air *chi*', the vital energy which accompanies the incoming air. Nor is this energy led into the physical beating heart but into a region similar to the Chinese *tantien*. Secondly, the Christian mystic, like the Sufi, is given a prayer, something as a focus for his or her feelings.

Another aspect of Sufi methods is well worth speaking about in connection with Pakua and Taoism: the 'turning' or 'whirling' of the Mevlevi and other dervish orders. The Mevlevi were founded by Jellaleddin Rumi in the 13th century. A dervish of this order takes part in a ritual that consists of turning about one's axis, right hand raised towards heaven, and left hand lowered towards earth.

> The right hand of the dervish is upturned towards heaven and accepts divine blessing, which passes through the heart and is transmitted to the world through the downward-pointing left hand. The dervishes look continually at the thumb of that downward hand; for them, it forms a vital fixed point which keeps the head clear and the senses alert.

> (*The Whirling Dervishes – A Commemoration*,
> International Rumi Committee, 1974: essay by Jeffrey Somers)

The ceremony is accompanied by inspiring music and watched over by the Sheikh or spiritual leader. As the dervishes turn about their own physical axes, they each form part of a larger circle which gradually turns, so that they make small circles within the larger. It is said that there is a relationship between their turning and the movement of celestial bodies.

Laleh Bakhtiar in his book *Sufi* (Thames & Hudson, London, 1976) writes:

> Static geometry is the geometry of lines, whereas dynamic forms are expressions of points. Each descent from the Divine Essence is a nuptial union, a conjunction of two opposites, active and passive, with a view to the production of a third. . . . The polarization which is expressed in geometry through static and dynamic forms corresponds exactly to the inseparable pairs of complementary spiritual stations between which the seeker constantly moves.

The author then lists the names of these 'stations', among which are:

contraction – expansion (*qabd* – *bast*)
gathering – separation (*jam* – *tafriqah*)

These are not unlike the Chinese expression referred to in Chapter 7:

expanding – gathering (*k'ai* – *ho*)

Gurdjieff, as reported by PD Ouspensky in the book *In Search of the Miraculous*, spoke about the 'two opposite' and the 'third' referred to in the above passage by Bakhtiar. He said,

> According to real, exact knowledge, one force, or two forces, can never produce a phenomenon. The presence of a third force is necessary, for it is only with the help of a third force that the first two can produce what can be called a phenomenon, no matter in what sphere. The teaching of the three forces is at the root of all ancient systems.

Bakhtiar presents the reader with diagrams from Islamic art and architecture together with explanations of their inner meaning. One cannot help but draw comparisons with Taoist diagrams that show the movements of Taoists during their meditational motions.

It is believed that the founder of Pakua was influenced by such activities. Professor K'ang Ko-Wu discovered that Tung

Hai Ch'uan himself became a member of the Chuan Chen Taoist sect. One of their meditation rituals was to walk not only a circle, but also to follow the Yin-Yang diagram shown in figure 104. This practice was called Chuan Tien Tsun, which means Rotating in Worship of Heaven – an expression that immediately reminds one of the practice of the Mevlevi dervishes. As they walked they intoned sayings reminding them of Heaven and the Great Void. This repetition of words was used, it is said, to help them to focus on one thought and so escape the 'myriad thoughts'. The walking of the Yin-Yang symbol began with a circling of the perimeter three times, anticlockwise, beginning on the right side, facing north. The practitioner would then walk along the curving dividing line from north to south, and turn west to walk three times clockwise, before once again crossing the symbol through the curving dividing line.

In spite of the widely held belief that Tung used the Taoist figure-walking as a basis for Pakua, it remains no more than might be called a rational conclusion, and does not convince the most severe critics or the partisans of other theories. 'There is no proof!' they cry. Assuming K'ang's conclusions are correct, however, why did Tung use what is effectively a religious practice, or a practice from a Way, for a martial purpose? It seems in a sense a misuse of methods. But perhaps that is only because of our limited Western outlook on the subject. It could just as well be argued that Tung's Pakua did as much to lift students up to a better understanding and an improvement in character as it did to foster fighting.

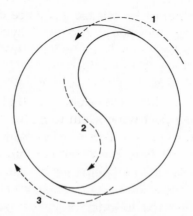

Figure 104 Taoist walking Yin-Yang diagram

I have come across nothing on the posture adopted, if any, by the Chuan Chen Taoists. It does seem likely, whatever the posture or postures might have been, that inwardly and accompanying the repetition of words, they endeavoured to guide or follow the *chi* along the *chinglo*, in conformity with the Taoist alchemical exercises that had existed for centuries. This too Tung Hai Ch'uan may have adopted. Certainly, Sun Lu Tang became preoccupied with such things.

Energy and the Mind

One of the questions that has intrigued me throughout my contact with the internal martial arts is whether the Forms cause – or are supposed to cause – any regular diversion of energy. By this I mean, does a Form of Pakua or Tai Chi Chuan cause, for instance, the blood supply to be increased or diminished to different parts of the body? Or one could ask if it does the same to the *chi*. In the case of Pakua, is the circle-walking representative of a real circulation of energy, *chi* or blood, as distinct from a theoretical one based solely on traditional thinking and unsupported by experimental proof? And do the different Palm Changes bring energy to a different part of the body in a regular, cyclic fashion? Intellectually it would be 'neat' if this type of thing did occur. But leaving aside one's sense of tidiness, are there any grounds for thinking that it might be so?

The popular Western attitude to physical training in the widest sense has changed over the last three decades. Expressions like 'psyching myself up' and the 'psychology of sport' are shorthand for the mental aspects that have received close attention. Athletes have reported unusual experiences when striving to reach a peak, or to go beyond their normal capacity. The consensus from these experiences is that the 'mind' can take the 'body' well past what seem to be the latter's possibilities. Prior to this recognition, Westerners on the whole relied on what was referred to as guts, determination, will-power, and similar descriptions of mental effort. In other words, it was accepted that you could always do more, do better, go further. But the subject of how to do so was not widely investigated. As a boy at school I remember jumping higher than I thought I could simply by giving myself a last-minute word of encouragement just as I began my run-up. I did not understand how – it just happened.

Alongside this, the increase in the knowledge of how the body works during strenuous activity has helped sports coaches. Probably everyone has heard of circuit training, in which several different efforts are made and then the whole cycle is repeated: for instance, running, climbing, jumping, vaulting, rolling, resting, and then beginning again. In this example the effort focuses respectively on the legs, the arms, the legs and abdomen, the whole body, and folding the body, before recuperating for a minute. There are many variations, but they all operate by transferring the muscular effort from one muscle group to another. By doing this, the different muscle groups have a period of rest before being activated again. The heart, lungs and circulation are called on throughout, and then given a period in which to recover. This is a Form of training, and it crudely fulfils the notion of circulating energy use in a specific pattern or cycle. But the aim is not specific. It is to promote athletic fitness: 'fitness' being defined as the speed with which the heart and lungs return to their normal level after making an effort.

To be incorporated in traditional Chinese martial arts training, circuit training would have had to be justified on the basis of the underlying theory and philosophy of Chi Kung (Qigong). If a sequence of movements did not accord with these theories, it was found unacceptable. There may be exceptions to this, but because there are hundreds (if not thousands) of Chinese Forms and systems I cannot be definite about it.

One of the basic tenets is that the Yang energy is encouraged to descend into the abdomen and legs, and the Yin energy to rise to the upper body. This is expressed in the hexagram of the

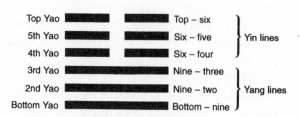

Figure 105 Tai diagram

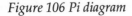

Figure 106 Pi diagram   *Figure 107 Horse stance*

I Ching known as the Tai Diagram: see figure 105. Fire is at the bottom and Water at the top. The opposite, the Pi Diagram, as in figure 106, shows the Fire, Yang, on top and the Water, Yin, at the bottom.

There are three ways in which this type of 'circulation' is achieved in Forms. One is to adopt a stance conducive to it. Par excellence, the horse stance is eminent for this: see figure 107. The solid, widely placed legs and the upright body indicate strength at the bottom and freedom at the top. Merely by standing in this posture, with no mental additional help, the tendency is for the Yang to go down and the Yin to ascend. This type of horse stance training was sometimes performed over long periods of time, so that the body was 'tamed' or 'trained' into submission.

A second way is to adopt the same or similar stances, and at the same time to mentally send the energy down into the abdomen and legs, and then up into the torso.

And finally, the third way is to mentally send the energy down and up at regular intervals throughout a Form, depending on which movement is being carried out.

There is a classical saying that 'the *i* (mind) directs the *chi* (vital energy) which directs the body'. This clearly shows that although an actual movement may be conducive to a change in *chi* energy direction, in the internal arts, at least, the mind (awareness, imagination, visualization, and so on) plays an important and probably indispensable role. Traditional theory maintains that correct performance leads to a revival of the

Pre-birth influences which benefit the student by correcting the Post-birth influences. A similar theory holds good for sitting (static) meditation.

Below are two examples of *chi* energy distribution patterns taken from Tai Chi Chuan. Having looked at them and having derived some principles from them, we can focus on some Pakua movements and treat them in a similar way.

Example 1

Beginning	*Chi* rises from *tantien* (lower abdomen)
Ward Off left	*Chi* sinks to *tantien*
Ward Off Right	*Chi* rises from *tantien*
Roll Back	*Chi* sinks to *tantien*
Press	*Chi* rises from *tantien*
Withdraw	*Chi* sinks to *tantien*
Push	*Chi* rises from *tantien*
Single Whip	*Chi* sinks to *tantien* and body turns to begin the Larger Heavenly Circulation.

This first sequence moves the *chi* through the Smaller Heavenly Circulation. It is followed by:

Lifting Hands	*Chi* spreads to whole body as arms open, and then focuses on mid-line (*Jen Mo*) at front of body
Shoulder Stroke	*Chi* moves to perineum. *Chi* now begins to move into Larger Heavenly Circulation
White Crane	*Chi* rises up *Jen Mo* to forehead
Turn from White Crane	*Chi* sinks to abdomen down *Jen Mo* and through pubic region to base of spine
Brush Left Knee	*Chi* rises from abdomen up spine (*Tu Mo*) to crown of head
Brush Right Knee	repeat
Brush Left Knee	repeat
Drive Monkey Away	*Chi* moves, with each complete movement, through the Larger Heavenly Circulation

Diagonal Flying	*Chi* spreads to whole body
Play Guitar	*Chi* focuses in *Jen Mo*
Shoulder Stroke	*Chi* moves to perineum

And so on through this Yang-style Form.

Example 2

The following information comes from the unpublished manuscript of a famous living Tai Chi master from China.

The *chi* movement is brought about almost entirely by 'mental instructions' or visualization: the theory is that the *chi* will follow the *i* (mind). Instructions begin with the advice to 'think' that each joint of the arms (beginning with the finger joints) 'stretches' – that is, that a space opens up between it and the next. This exercise facilitates and promotes the flow of *chi*.

For each movement to be performed, the order of joint use is described in meticulous detail, and the *i* (mind) is required to focus on a series of (acupuncture) points in a certain sequence.

Another aspect of this method assumes that the movement of one limb – for example, an arm – attracts the correspondingly appropriate movement of another limb; furthermore that the movements of one or two limbs automatically produce other movements in the remaining limbs.

The overall aim of this method is to distribute the *chi* to the various channels (*chinglo*) and points in a certain order.

The manuscript gives the impression of a teacher completely steeped in the Tai Chi tradition, someone whose sensitivity to movement and *chi* flow makes it possible for him to experience the description he is giving. It is beyond the reach of any beginner – in fact, I would say, of most Tai Chi practitioners. It illustrates a suggestion made elsewhere in this book (page 96–8) that we are not 'equal', that what is possible for one person may not be possible, at the time, for another.

What light do these examples throw on the opening question of this chapter – whether a Form in itself produces a definite cyclic or repeated energy flow. In the first example a traditional flow, or rather two, are said to be produced by specific movements of the Form. Roughly speaking, when an arm rises or both arms rise, the *chi* rises, either through the *Jen Mo* or *Tu Mo*, the *chinglo* which together circle the entire trunk and head in the sagittal front-to-back plane. When an arm sinks, the *chi* sinks.

If it should happen that one arm rises and the other arm sinks when, for example, the *chi* has risen, then it will be the descending arm that assists the *i* to cause the *chi* to sink. It *has* to sink; *it cannot rise indefinitely*.

If the *chi* is at the front, an arm moving back will take it to the back, and vice versa. It seems therefore that the practitioner has 'at the back of his or her mind' the two major traditional *chi* flow directions, and the Form is linked with these in the most appropriate manner.

A further important factor is the notion of 'opening and closing'. When the arms open before Lifting Hands or Play Guitar, the *chi* spreads to the whole body. When the arms close into the posture itself, the *chi* moves into the closed-off region – that is, the front of the body where the *Jen Mo chinglo* is.

Then there is the breath. Breath is used to reinforce the movement of *chi* and is best left as 'natural'. It is clear that when the body opens, the breath, the air, will come in, and when the body closes the breath will move with the *chi*, assist the *chi*. The movements of a Form which opens the thorax, lifts the chest, expands the upper back, will, if the Form is done in a relaxed state, encourage inhalation.

In the second and necessarily sketchy example the approach is far more detailed. Instead of a general flow of *chi* being established, the Form is approached like a complex treatment of acupuncture, shiatsu or moxibustion. How subjective this approach is it is hard to say. Mainly, it illustrates for us a possible development in sensitivity to movement and internal energy.

Pakua

If you have seen someone sitting in meditation with eyes open, or seen a statue of the Buddha with his eyes almost closed, you will have received an impression of someone with the eyes on one thing but the awareness on something else. Likewise, in Pakua, the eyes are on the index finger but much of the awareness is elsewhere. Should the directing of *chi* be a part of Pakua training in a similar way to that of Tai Chi, the most prominent question would be that of speed. It is much easier to imagine the guiding of *chi* flow when moving at very low speeds than it is to imagine it when moving at high speed.

In Tai Chi the movement is continuous and without explosive, focused delivery of energy, or *ching*, except when engaged in Push Hands. When *ching* occurs in Push Hands, the martial arts theory is that energy has been accumulated in the *tantien* and is then issued through the palms on to the body of the partner. This is outside the scope of this book, in which we are emphasizing the meditative aspects.

We can therefore regard the flow of *chi* in a similar way to how it is understood in Tai Chi – with one important exception. This centres on the expression 'coiling energy' (or 'spiralling energy'). Coiling energy is found more prominently in Chen-style Tai Chi than in the other styles, although it is mainly a question of emphasis rather than of the complete absence of such energy. In Pakua, coiling energy plays an important role. It is implied in the coiling, dragon-like movements of the body, and can indeed be experienced. To my knowledge there are no such coiling *chinglo* or channels in the traditional charts and models of Traditional Chinese Medicine. The type of coiling energy depicted in figure 108 are closer to the action of *ching* than *chi*. So a noteworthy distinction appears here. Stimulating or depressing the flow of *chi* along natural pathways is one type of activity, but converting and using energy, *ching*, is another. A useful but limited analogy might be the presence of energy bio-

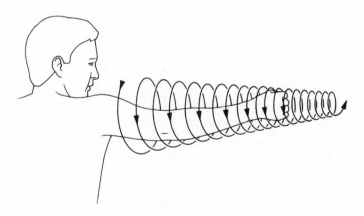

Figure 108 Coiling energy diagram

chemicals in the body, along with the presence of oxygen, being likened to *chi*, and the conversion and use of those ingredients into work or action of an unspecified nature being likened to *ching*. In both the instance of *chi* and the instance of basic ingredients there are recognized places, channels and processes that are illustrated in books on physiology and acupuncture, but in the instance of *ching* and energy release there are countless variations.

The coiling energy of different martial arts in which it is emphasized is thus not as well 'mapped' as that of the flow of *chi*. The experience of coiling energy, too, is highly subjective. It varies considerably from student to student. If you practise the forms and basic coiling, twisting, and turning movements of the art, you will begin to recognize what is meant.

To make this even clearer, look at figure 109. In this exercise, which is given merely for purposes of illustration, the student begins in a knees-bent posture, turned to left or right at the waist. As the student rises, a turn is made in the opposite direction, the hands and arms turn as in the movement Dragon Turns Its Head, first in one direction and then the other. Coiling can be directly experienced. Then reverse the exercise, descending to the original beginning posture. Forms of Chi Kung are based on this type of movement.

Although the body is of course working through the normal joints, such as the elbows and the knees, all of which are hinge joints, and although the *chi* flow is moving as usual down the recognized *chinglo*, the overall result is different from the sum of the parts. The overall result is one closer to that of a serpent or dragon – an animal with a different joint structure.

Figure 109 Coiling exercise

Turning to the question of meditation in movement – or rather, awareness in movement – the suggestion is that when practising the Pakua Forms, you should move slowly, deliberately, with relaxation, and try to be aware of this coiling activity. In my own view, such training would be helped by a basic ability in Tai Chi. I say this because there is difficulty in being aware of one's body when it is moving, and because of the contribution that Tai Chi can make towards the development of such awareness. A large part of this development is the cultivation of relaxation. Tension blocks off awareness just as pressure on a vein blocks off blood flow. The movements of Pakua are much more conducive to tension than are the movements of Yang-style Tai Chi for example, and so the difficulties are greater. If you are unwilling to undertake basic Tai Chi training, compensate by doing your Pakua very slowly.

Chapter 13

Ways of the Dragon: Applications of Pakua

In its twisting, circling, turning, rising and falling movements, Pakua is very often linked with the movements, the power and the changing qualities of the dragon. The form presented in this book has dragon movements at the beginning and end of each Palm Change. This mythical animal played a prominent role in the many ceremonies carried out by the Emperor, priests and officials of the court of China. It is a symbol of change, transformation and great flexibility. If we want to enter into the spirit of the dragon it is helpful to know some of the beliefs associated with it.

The Chinese saw the world as a number of kingdoms whose influence and power was governed by dragons. The year was divided into twelve moons. In the fifth moon when the ground was dry and parched, dragon dances were held with as many as 12 men taking part to carry and dance under the makeshift body. Water was sprinkled on the creature to invite it to produce rain. Firecrackers were ignited, gongs beaten, and noises of all types made to summon the vital downpour. It was in the sixth moon that the king of dragons, Lung Wang, assembled his dragon hosts and told them to bring rain to the parched earth. In a mainly agricultural society, a creature that brought rain to the earth was revered and remembered. During the reign of Huang Ti, around 2500 BC, it was reported that the first 'true dragon' appeared. It had the horns of a stag, the head of a camel, the ears of a cow, the neck of a snake, the scales of a fish, the claws of an eagle, and the paws of a tiger.

As time passed, more and more dragons appeared in stories and legends. One feature of the dragon was its amazing eyesight. It could see a single blade of grass from a great distance away. In this connection it is interesting to note that the word *dragon* is etymologically akin to the Greek *drakein*, which means 'to gaze' or 'to see'. The king of dragons, Lung Wang, embodied the masculine or Yang principle. The Emperor himself was called the True Dragon, rising above ordinary mortals. His throne was the Dragon Seat, his pen the Dragon's Brush. In the Ming dynasty his standard bore a red dragon, and under the Manchu a gold dragon.

The dragon sometimes hides in the deepest caverns or in remote mountains, or coils up in the depth of the sea. When the time is right, it stirs, slowly, conscious of its power. It swims from the depths, parting the waters, rising amid foam, and soars up into the storm clouds. Its claws dart down the forked lightning, its scales writhe in the whirlpools and glisten like the bark of rainswept pine trees. When it speaks, it speaks as the hurricane of later winter and as the herald of springtime. Its breath is vapour, water, fire. It changes its nature: it is the spiritual dragon of the wind and rain, then it is the dragon of hidden treasures that mortals cannot see. In the form of the Yellow Dragon it taught humankind to write.

A 'hidden dragon' is a great man whom the world has not yet recognized. He is a man who waits for his own time to come. When it does, he begins to distinguish himself, and others feel his presence. Slowly, people come to him for guidance. He is cautious, like someone crossing a flooded river. At last he sees his way clearly, as a dragon ascending into the heavens. Even then he is cautious, for pride and arrogance can bring a fall. He remembers the Yin side of his nature and yields to its wisdom. Although he is in the heavens of his destiny he remembers the womb of his creation. He feels the sky and sees the earth: the freedom of the one and the limitations of the other. He knows his purpose and his nature – to change and be changed – and so, following his nature and understanding it, he remains. Nothing can conquer him, for he is no one thing.

Many years ago when I was interested in Judo, I bought a book on something called Judo-do, a European invention that claimed to be better than Judo. Some of the illustrations of the throwing techniques were very intriguing. It looked as though the opponent had to stand still while the person who was to make the throw went for a long, circuitous walk and eventually arrived behind him, finally to carry out the throw. I was pleased to read later in a Judo magazine that the Budokwai Judo Club (the British Judo Association) had sent a team across the English Channel and soundly thrashed the Judo-do aficionados. During the same period there were various other books purporting to define one or other 'martial art' but that contained such crude notions of retaliatory violence as to suggest overwhelming force on the part of the victor or dumb inertia on the part of the loser. Certainly, some of the applications taught and illustrated in modern books and magazines are completely impractical due to the elaborate movements involved. They require a sort of languor or passivity on the part of the opponent that is totally unrealistic. Other applications would be best left in the instruction manuals of the SAS or Green Berets. What I want to illustrate in this book are basic, and to a certain extent obvious, uses of Pakua, originating quite simply from its rotating, sinuous forms. These do not have as a prerequisite a passive opponent, nor are they in themselves patently deadly. A martial arts technique depends on the selectivity of the user, not on the movement itself.

By now, if you have followed the instructions, you will have a reasonably clear notion of the fundamental movements of Pakua. With combat in mind, you can appreciate that a rotating, travelling object – that is, a person – is less easy to hold, hit, deflect, or stop than one that is travelling in a straight line. Secondly, Pakua stresses change and movement, that is, plenty of stepping. This implies that if you are stepping and moving you will have a larger number of openings than someone who confronts an opponent face to face, like two old-time prize-fighters. In the annals of Pakua combat, it occurred comparatively frequently that when fighting a Pakua practitioner an opponent could not 'lay a glove on him', as the saying goes. When the attack from the Pakua man came it did so out of the blue. So, evasion and lightning attacks are the two key words for us. These are characteristics of the dragon.

Let us look at this with a few simple examples. In figure 110 one man aims a punch at the face of another: man on the left (L) strikes at man on the right (R). R steps to his right as if beginning to walk the circle, and to be on the safe side raises his arms in a dragon posture: figure 111. His rising arm may parry the punch if within range, but the footwork may be enough to keep him out of range.

Figure 110 Punch to face   *Figure 111 Walking circle parry*

Continuing the same sequence: suppose the defender R wants to strike back. He does not have to withdraw his right arm and start to hit with it. His Pakua training will have taught him to continue the parrying movement into a striking movement – say, to the jaw or to the side of the face, as in figure 112.

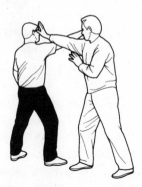

Figure 112 Dragon posture used to strike

Continuing the same sequence: if the initial attacker L turns to face R, R is continuing to walk a segment of the circle as if to get behind L. He does not succeed because L is turning, but his walk takes him perhaps further round to the rear of L, and he strikes towards the back of the head, as in figure 113. Remember that R has trained to strike on the move, in contrast to some martial arts which teach students to take up a stance in order to strike. After a first strike, R *continues to move*. This is an important distinction, and a strong feature, of Pakua.

Figure 113 Walking circle to get behind opponent (two views)

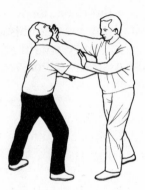

Figures 114 and 115 Counter attack using Third Palm Change

Another example could be one in which L grabs at R. L's angle of attack is directly forwards. R uses his left forearm to knock or push aside L's arms, stepping with his left foot to his left and bringing his right arm across, using the palm to strike L on the head: see figure 114.

You may remember that this is the opening move of the third Palm Change, stepping away from the centre for the first time in an initial movement. If you were to treat the Palm Change as a complete attacking and defending technique, you would then crouch down, turning quickly to your left, and strike your opponent in the lower abdominal region, as in figure 115. In doing so you would turn your back on your opponent. This is a controversial move in martial arts circles. The argument on one side is that you should never turn your back because you can-

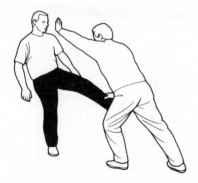

Figure 116 Counter attack using
Fifth Palm Change

Figure 117 Palm change used

not see your opponent. The other side is that you do this very quickly and it is totally unexpected, and furthermore that you have already hit your opponent once and he is off balance or hurt.

With experience you will begin to see genuinely martial applications for the movements of the Palm Changes.

For instance, the movement described below is from the fifth Palm Change. One application is in the event that an opponent launches a kick. You step back with your right foot, palming down the kick with your right hand and striking to the face with your left palm, as in figures 116 and 117. Another more spectacular technique is derived from the eighth Palm Change, that of the Lion holds ball: figure 118. This is a move found in wrestling styles and also in Judo (in the Shoulder Wheel technique). An attacker grabs at you or stretches out his right arm to hit. If you are able to seize him by the wrist or cloth of his jacket, you duck under the arm you are holding, as in figure 119, and push your other arm between his legs, pulling him towards you, as in figure 120. Turning your body away from him, you settle him on your shoulders and tip him away to your left or dump him on his back in front of you: figures 121 and 122. Of course the same technique can be used simply as a parry and strike: figure 123.

A snake technique from the Palm Changes involves turning round to meet an attack. A blow comes from behind, on the right side: figure 124. You turn, raising your right arm bent, and parry the blow: figure 125, then follow up with a chop, using

Figure 118 Lion holds a ball

Figure 119 Beginning to use Lion

*Figure 120 Using Lion palm change
(i)*

*Figure 121 Using Lion palm change
(ii)*

*Figure 122 Using Lion palm change
(iii)*

*Figure 123 Lion palms to parry and
strike*

Figure 124 Using Snake technique (i)   *Figure 125 Using Snake technique (ii)*

Figure 126 Using Snake technique (iii)

the parrying arm: figure 126. This can be followed by a blow with the other arm, or a kick.

These few examples should make it clear that Pakua is a practical martial art. If you decide to practise such applications, start by using very light attacks. Give your partner plenty of time to block and counter, and above all focus at first on getting the Pakua techniques right. It is not the most important thing in the beginning to stop the blow or grab. That is why the attacks at this stage should be using almost no force. Then no one will be hurt. If no one is going to be hurt, the defender has no reason to feel tense from fear of being hurt. He or she can practise almost as though training alone. The techniques will be more accurate. When they are accurate, the attacks can be harder and more realistic. Some people argue that attacks should always be tough so that the defender learns from hard knocks. There is something to be said for this – but I don't recommend it: that is more applicable to self-defence training, pure and simple.

If you are not familiar with any martial arts training, a few pointers may be useful to minimise the risk of injury and make your training more effective.

1) When you move, your whole body moves. If you parry a blow, do not just stick your arm out. This is weak. It also may hurt your arm much more than a whole body movement.

2) When you strike, if the training exercise is focusing on one move, do not stop, rigidly, as you finish the move. Also, do not fall out of the fighting mode and let your arms drop to your sides prior to trying again. Both of these habits give you bad habits! Always go on with a few continuous movements, as if your main technique were part of a chain of techniques.

3) Whenever you can, keep your eyes focused on the whole of your partner's body, not just his attacking arm or foot. Unless you do this you will be unable to see what the other limbs are doing.

4) *Move like a dragon!*

Conclusion

You should now have a good grasp of the type of material to be found in the world of Pakua. Of course each aspect described in this book can be elaborated on, and more examples and detail discovered. Different teachers emphasize different sides and styles of the art according to their background and choice. But of course this does not cancel out in any way the foundation we have laid down. The eight Palm Changes are basic, and as such are more important than anything that follows. The first Palm Change is basic to the other seven, and as such is in turn more important than anything that follows.

Remember that circles and circling are pre-eminent. Foot-work uses whole circles or parts of circles. Body and arm work use circles in three dimensions which turn the movements into spirals and coils. When these several spirals and circles mesh together, the body moves like a well-oiled machine – better, because there can be those added animal and human touches of gracefulness, of dynamic nuance. If the performer is so moved, a martial spirit can pervade these same actions.

You, your ego, cannot dominate the circle or the spiral. If anything you are dominated by, or rather submitted to, it. It can teach you if you let it. Correct movement therefore comes first. Repetition of a movement, aiming at good joint use and circularity, can gradually penetrate your body and your attitude so that both change and become 'happy'. Speed is not a primary concern. Speed develops from correctness. In fact, correctness eventually produces speed, from fluency: speed will simply appear. As a famous judo master once put it, mastery is not self-conscious – in the usual meaning of that expression. Pakua or judo or aikido technique cannot be mastered. You gradually become more and more at one with them. So you must build from correctness.

If you were ever to reach a level in which you were at one with the concepts of Pakua, then the moment could appear when you naturally filled it with your own true subjectivity, your own Pre-birth and Post-birth essential qualities. But we have to agree that this is a remote thing, inspirational for the future rather than an immediate possibility.

Applying the *Kua*, the trigrams, and their Yin-Yang combinations to your body movements and attitudes can be a help. Such attempts at application as we can make will serve to stimulate interest. Breaking movement down into Yin and Yang in varying degrees and applying them to three levels: legs, lower torso, upper torso and shoulders and head, can focus attention on what the body is doing and the tensions and relaxations involved. Putting these analyses back together again in an attempt at synthesis continues to add interest. The whole resulting movement then merges such attempts into a continuous sequence which only well-developed attention is able to follow.

Moving quite slowly and emphasizing the meditative aspect inherent in Pakua can open up a deeper world of relaxation and natural breathing, bringing a quietness that everyone should welcome. Focusing on the spirit of each animal, to whatever extent one can, and attempting to imbue one's movement with that spirit can show us new fields of feeling previously unexplored. For this to prosper, we need respect – not fearful respect but the simple reverential respect that more and more people today feel towards the natural world. This is an exercise in itself – to think about the planet, the rain forests, the environment – and then do some movements in a way that expresses these thoughts and the feelings they evoke.

Western enquiry, such as Craniosacral Therapy, can increase one's knowledge of what is going on in one's body and to some extent one's awareness or interpretation of sensations. To watch dancers or martial artists from other styles can also reveal or mirror things which, left to one's own devices, one might never discover.

In the modern West we have only recently begun to be able to 'think' in a way that has been practised for centuries in China, where the fundamental and obvious changes in life have been observed and afforded something of the obvious significance that they deserve. For instance, if we could speak to a tree and ask it the question, 'what is the nature of water?', it might reply, 'The nature of water is to bring food and life.' Having no brain like ours, it would verbalize in this instance only its direct experience of water. There could be no theory. Unlike us humans, a tree has no psychological barrier between it and the rest of the universe. Its experience is direct.

It does appear that human beings were themselves at one time more directly in contact with the earth and possibly with the processes of their own lives. Pakua can be a means of renewing that contact, starting with making contact with oneself. Making contact must also be the fundamental reason for meditation. So if you wish to continue to study Pakua and find a teacher, I suggest you follow certain guidelines.

Look for a means, as you study, of deepening your awareness. Secondly, look for a feeling of respect for what you are doing and for a feeling which I can only call 'happiness'. In a class situation this may be difficult. The teacher may be emphasizing something which he or she believes to be important, and as a pupil you have to go along with it. It may not conform to what you want, but the whole class cannot change to suit you. Pakua teachers are not found on every street corner, yet, so make the most of what you can find, and use it to help your own aim. Whatever a pupil or teacher may have made of Pakua, its source, the *I Ching*, is a sound and tested one. The Yin-Yang principle is a sound and tested principle. So in a class, what you may have to do is to tease out what is sound and what is a deviation.

Do not be overly impressed by a teacher's wide knowledge of Forms. A teacher may know a lot of information and a lot of Pakua movements. But the movements are nothing more nor less than expressions of a principle and an idea. Circles and spirals are everywhere. But can you make even one Palm Change and express these figures perfectly, or near perfectly? If you cannot and do not try to study this, then to know many, many movements can simply lead you up a blind alley.

Although you may not be attracted to the martial side of Pakua, at least give it a try. There is something demanded by the act of having to defend yourself, even in a class situation, which nothing else can give you. You *have* to focus, you *have* to get it together, you *have* to look and move and defend: it is an immediate necessity. At the same time it does not require tension, fear, or anything negative. Defending yourself can be a clear, clean, decisive action, leaving no hard feelings but perhaps a few bruises. It will pull all your body together like nothing else.

The most important item of clothing in Pakua is footwear. Get some thin-soled shoes with firm-fitting uppers. The entire sole of the shoe should rest on the floor when you put your foot down. You do not want shoes which have a toe turning up off the ground. Trainers are too thick and cumbersome. The upper should not impede your ankle movement in any way. Then for the rest, tracksuit or loose clothing will do fine. You do not need a Kung Fu outfit.

If you can, find at least one kindred spirit with whom you can talk and try things out. Let this partner watch you and say how he or she sees what you do. It is rare for anyone to be able to take a look at how he or she moves with impartiality. If you have access to a video camera, tape yourself moving. The first time I saw myself moving on tape was a big shock to me. I had been only dimly aware of certain characteristics of my movements, and then I saw these things as plain as day on the screen – it told me a lot about myself.

Pakua is in its infancy in the West, especially in Europe. It is a lusty infant even so. The chances are that as it spreads and grows, a number of things will happen. This prediction is based on what happened to Judo, later Karate, then Kung Fu, and more recently to Tai Chi Chuan. It will become more commercial. It will feature in competitions. It will produce teachers of very widely differing levels of skill and knowledge. It will be subjected to watering down, incorrect tuition as well as correct tuition, and movements will be introduced into it which at present play no part in it. In some instances it will veer so far away from the Pakua path that even if Tung Hai Ch'uan himself were to reappear from the grave he would not recognize his creation. Some students will learn good Pakua and hone their skills to a high level, and pockets of such dedicated people will persist. In time, most of the Pakua available will have taken the shape of a Westernized Chinese martial art. Nothing can be done about all this; no one can hold back the tides of change. It is simply up to each individual to try to absorb the fundamentals and keep them alive.

A final piece of advice is about mixing things up. It is tempting, on seeing a similarity between, say, a movement from Tai Chi and a movement from Pakua, to try to merge them. There is nothing wrong with this provided you do not forget the original. Make notes and sketches and diagrams that can serve as a record of what you once did. As you change, along with your Pakua performance, you will find that you cut corners and forget. If you keep no records, you will find one day that, try as you may, you are unable to do a certain group of movements in the way you were taught or originally learned. This original way, this Form number one, might have been less skilful and sophisticated than the way you now do it, but it might have contained some essential ingredient you overlooked at that time – and this may be an ingredient you now need.

Appendix

Complete Eight Palm Changes

FIRST CHANGE

SECOND CHANGE

Walking anticlockwise repeat the first four moves of the First Change.
Now perform the following moves.

Finally, repeat the last four moves of the First Change.

THIRD CHANGE

Walking clockwise repeat the first move of the First Change.
Now perform the following moves.

Finally, step clockwise along the circle, right hand high.

FOURTH CHANGE

Walking clockwise repeat the first move of the First Change.
Now perform the following moves.

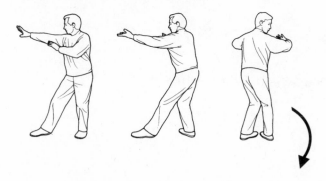

Finally, repeat the last four moves of the First Change.

FIFTH CHANGE

Repeat the first two moves of the First Change. Now perform the following moves.

SIXTH CHANGE

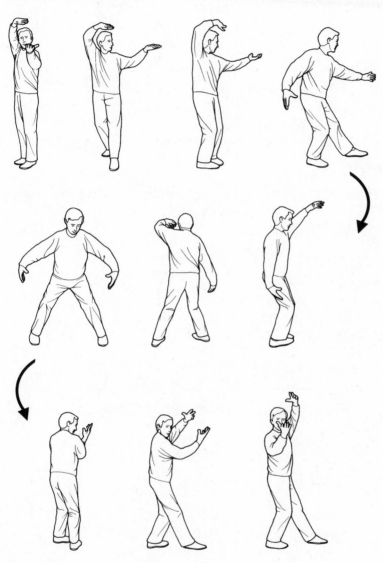

SEVENTH CHANGE

Walking clockwise repeat the first movement of the First Change.

Now perform the following moves.

EIGHTH CHANGE

Walking clockwise repeat the first movement of the First Change.

Now perform the following moves.

Finally, repeat the last four movements of the First Change.

Glossary of Terms

Animals – the eight animals whose movements are used in Pakua as basic examples: snake, dragon, lion, hawk, bear, phoenix, unicorn, monkey.

Cerebrospinal fluid – liquid that surrounds the spinal cord and brain and maintains an undulating pressure, and also carries nutrients as well as removing waste products.

Chi – vital energy, vitality, intrinsic natural energy circulating throughout the body (*Qi*).

Ching – *chi* energy converted into external action energy. Concentrated *chi* used externally.

Eight Palm Changes – the fundamental movements or changes used in Pakua.

Endorphin – 'the morphine within': pain-subduing substances occurring naturally in the body.

Feng Shui – Chinese geomancy used to understand the energetic relationships between all classes of objects and natural phenomena and their effects on human beings.

Five Elements – five fundamental phases through which all phenomena pass: metal, wood, fire, earth, water.

Form – in martial arts a sequence of movements laid down by the style or school concerned. The Eight Palm Changes are a Form: each single Change is also a Form in that it contains a sequence of movements.

Greater Circulation – a route followed by the *chi* through the body and a focus for certain meditation methods. Sometimes called Larger Heavenly Circulation.

Hara – Japanese equivalent of Chinese *tantien*, a point in the lower abdomen corresponding to centre of gravity. Also a focus of *chi* (*Qi*).

Hsing-I – form of Chinese boxing or Kung Fu – 'Body-Mind Boxing'.

I Ching – the Book of Changes: a book of divination using the trigrams combined into hexagrams of six lines.

Inertia – the tendency of a body to stay where it is or to continue moving unchanging in the direction it is moving in.

K'ai-ho – principle of 'expanding and collecting'.

Lesser Circulation – a route followed by the *chi* through the body and a focus for certain meditation methods. Sometimes called Smaller Heavenly Circulation.

Momentum – the speed and force of an object in motion.

Qi – see *Chi*.

Shaolin – name of Chinese Temple ('small forest') in which many martial arts are said to have originated.

Shen – spiritual energy: the highest energy produced in a human being.

Swivel – turning on one or both feet without breaking contact with the floor.

T step – foot position in which the heel of one foot is at right-angles to the instep of the other foot.

Tai Chi Chuan – a system of slow, meditative exercises.

Tao Te Ching – seminal Taoist book attributed to the sage Lao-tzu.

Taoism – one of the major schools of Chinese philosophy and religion; an important aspect is to be natural, at one with nature and universal law.

Trigram – three lines, broken or unbroken in different combinations signifying Yin and Yang.

Tung Hai Ch'uan – founder of Pakua.

V step – foot position in which the toes of both feet are turned in to make a V shape.

Yang – the male, hard, positive aspect of any phenomenon. A harder movement.

Yin – the female, soft, negative aspect of any phenomenon. A softer movement.

Yin-che – Taoist hermits: those who 'obscure themselves'.

Further Reading

Blackmer, Joan Dexter, *Acrobats of the Gods*, Inner City Books, New York, 1989

Cohen, Don, *An Introduction to Craniosacral Therapy*, North Atlantic, California, 1995

Crandall, Joseph, Classical Pakua Translations, Smiling Tiger, California

Crompton, Paul, *Five Steps*, PHC Ltd, London and New York, 1996

Fung Yu-Lan, *A Short History of Chinese Philosophy*, Macmillan, London, 1948

Goldberg, Jeff, *Anatomy of a Scientific Discovery*, (a study of endorphins), Bantam, London, 1988

Li Zi Ming, *Liang Zheng Pu Eight Diagram Palm*, High View Publications, California, 1993

Liang Shou-Yu, Yang Jwing-Ming & Wu Chen-Ching, *Baguazhang*, YMAA, Boston, 1994

Olson, Stuart Alve, *Intrinsic Energies of Tai Chi Chuan*, Dragon Door Publications, Minnesota, 1994

Park Bok Nam, *Fundamentals of Pa Kua Chang* vols 1 & 2, High View Publications, California, 1993 and 1996

Smith, Robert, and Pittman, Allen, *Pakua – Eight Trigram Boxing*, Tuttle, Vermont, 1990

Wilhelm, Richard (translator), *I Ching – the Book of Changes*, Routledge, London, 1951

Useful Addresses

The following is a list of Pakua instructors in different countries. The author is not in a position to comment on the methods or standing of any of these instructors at the present time. The list is for information only and should be seen as a starting-point. It is accurate as we go to print.

Great Britain

Bolwell, John P, 4, Carpenters Way, Turfhill, Rochdale, OL16 4XU
Crompton, Paul H, 102 Felsham Road, London, SW15 1DQ
Hines, Edward, 55 Manor Drive, Leeds, LS6 1DD
Nagle, Patrick, 83 Elizabeth Road, London, E6 1BW
Nicholls, Jerry D, 11 Vastern Road, Reading, RG1 8DJ
Townsend, Damon, 5 Harley Avenue, Bolton, BL2 5RN

Canada

(City, State and Telephone numbers available only in some instances.)
Babin, Michael, Ottawa, Ontario, 613 567 3120
James, Andrew, Toronto, Ontario, 416 465 6122
Kwok Chan, Kingston, Ontario, 613 546 2116
Smith, Michael, 651 2 Road, Richmond, British Columbia, 604 241 0172
Tuttle, Eric, 346 1/2 Princess Street, Kingston, Ontario, 613 542 9025
Wang, Alec, Vancouver, British Columbia, 604 251 1809

United States

Allen, Frank, 342 E. 9th Street, New York, NY 10003. 212 533 1751
Black, Vince, P.O. Box 36235, Tucson, Arizona, 85740. 602 544 4838
Bracy, John, 151 Kalmus, M–7–B, Costa Mesa, CA 92626. 714 557 8959
Cartmell, Tim, Westminster, CA 714 896 9531

Choi, Wai Lun, 2054 West Irving Park Road, Chicago, IL 60618. 312 472 3331

Cohen, Kenneth, PO Box 234, Nederland, CO 80466. 303 258 0971

Dale, Andrew, PO Box 77040, Seattle, WA 09133. 206 283 0055

Eshelman, Larry, 2814 Broad Avenue, Altoona, PA 16602. 814 941 9998

Fong, Bryant, PO Box 210159, San Francisco, CA 94121. 415 753 3838

Gracenin, Nick, 28 North Pine Street, Sharon, PA 16146. 412 983 1126

Guerin, Glenn, 134 E. Kings Highway, Shreveport, LA 71104. 318 865 3578

Johnson, Jerry Alan, PO Box 52144, Pacific Grove, CA 93950. 408 646 9399

Mark, Bow Sim, 246 Harrison Avenue, Boston, MA 02111. 617 426 0958

Miller, Dan, PO Box 51967, Pacific Grove, CA 93950. 408 622 0789

Painter, Dr John, 1514 E. Abram St, Arlington, TX 76010. 817 860 0129

Pittman, Allen, 2810 Dunnington Circle, Chamblee, GA 30341. 404 270 1642

Ralston, Peter, 6601 Telegraph Ave., Oakland, CA 94609. 415 658 0802

For further information refer to martial arts and New Age magazines; Tai Chi instructors often know of Pakua instructors.

Index

acupuncture (channels) 18
Aikido 8–9, 27
alchemy 95, 99
animals 4, 27, 40, 41–6
animals (list of) 41
arm positions 58
Art of Walking the Circle 2
attention vii, ix, 1
awareness 88

balance 24
biofeedback 25
brain waves vii
breathing viii

Centre (The) 35–40
centrifugal force 33
cerebrospinal fluid 17–21
Chang Chao Tung 12
Changes 61
  first 61,
  second 65
  third 66,
  fourth 68,
  fifth 61,
  sixth 73,
  seventh 76,
  eighth 81
Cheng T'ing Hua 8
Chen 1
Cheng Man Ching 27
chi 1, 11, 15, 25, 53, 98, 118, 123 ff
Chi Kung 9, 25, 41, 123 ff
Chiang Jung Ch'iao 10
ching 118, 133
chinglo 18
Chinese martial arts 1, 2, 9
Chuang-tzu 116–17
Circle (The) 33–40, 54
circuit training 128
circulation 24, 25, 129
coiling energy 133

combat 139 ff
Confucius 92, 93
cranial osteopathy 17–21

dervishes 124–5
dragon 27, 116, 135, 136–44
dragon (types of) 43–4
Dragon Turns Its Head 30

Eight Ultimates 1
Eight Palm Changes 2
endorphins 22–3

Feng Shui 11, 41
Five Elements 94, 119
Forms 121
Frantzis, Bruce Kumar 28
Fung Yu Lan 93

Gurdjieff 94, 95, 125

hawk 41
homeostasis 18
Hsing-I 1, 4, 13, 39

I-Ching 3–4, 10, 103–15, 129

Ji Jian Cheng 3–4, 9, 14, 28, 56
Judo 137

K'ang Ko-Wu 7, 125
k'ai-ho 100, 101, 125
Koichi Tohei 27

Lesser Heavenly Circulation 31
  (alternative names
  & description of) 123 ff
Liu Hsin 92
Liu Yun Ch'iao 28
Lion Holding a Ball 30

Ma Wei-Chih 8

mantra vii
Martha Graham 2, 4
martial 2
meditation vii–5
meditation (Taoist) 116–22
monkey 27
morphine 22

neurotransmitters 22

Old Fu style 51
organs (of the body) 42

Pa-Chi 1
Painter, Dr. John 28
Pakua (definition of) 2
Palm Changes 41, 53, 54–85, 105, 106, 111
Philokalia 124
psychosoma viii

sages 6
sensation viii
Shaolin 6
shen 98, 118
sifu 13
Single Palm Change 52
skull 17
spine 15–21
spinning 64
spiral diagram 33–4
straight lines 39
stretch reflex 23

Sufis 123
sutures (of skull) 17
stress 26
Sun Lu Tang 9, 12, 28, 56, 111

T step 29, 47–53
Tai Chi Chuan 1–4, 13, 30, 47, 63, 88, 89, 101, 122, 130–1
tantien 35, 36, 53, 123 ff
Taoism 92
Taoist meditation 116–22
trigrams 103–15
trigrams (names in Pakua) 103–5
trigrams (and parts of body) 108
Tung Hai Ch'uan 6–8, 96, 125
Twelve Terrestrial Branches 43

Upanishads 26
Uyeshiba 27

V step 29, 47–53, 112–13

Yang 1, 24, 117, 128
Yang Chu 93
Yang Jwing-Ming 11
Yin 1, 24, 117, 128
Yin-Yang 92, 101, 102, 106–8, 112–15, 126
Yin Fu 8
Yin Shih Tzu 15

Zen 26